soundprints contemporary composers

canadian 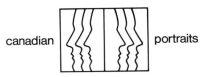 portraits

soundprints

contemporary composers **peter such**

clarke, irwin & company limited/toronto/vancouver

© 1972 by Clarke, Irwin & Company Ltd.

ISBN 0 7720 0564 8

1 2 3 4 5 6   77 76 75 74 73 72

Printed in Canada

to nina   who taught Ljuba how to dance

musically speaking, Canada has not yet come of age. I hope this statement will irritate many of those Canadians who feel that Canada is *already* musically mature, with our excellent orchestras, outstanding chamber groups, top-notch music schools and world-renowned singers, pianists, and so on.

Not so. An artistically mature community (call it a nation) has its *own* art, its *own* literature, its *own* music, to draw upon; moreover it has an active awareness of the creative utterance of its artists, and in addition it has the capacity to discriminate between the phony and the genuine. By and large, Canadian audiences have yet to develop this sense of ''our-own-ness''. To most Canadian audiences, musical ''culture'' has to do with Beethoven, Bach, Brahms and other great masters of European musical literature. But, to put it unkindly, no amount of listening to the music of dead Germans, especially those who have been safely certified as ''masters'', will impart to the Canadian music-lover that power of sensitive discrimination which is the hallmark of the truly cultivated person. Brahms and Beethoven wrote masterworks which all of us should know, to be sure, but they tell us far more about their *own* time and place than they tell us of ours. Obviously. ''But'' you say, ''the music of Bach and Beethoven is timeless!'' Nonsense! Do we really believe that 3,000 years from now the world will be as aware as we are of Beethoven and Bach, even with the blessings of print and recordings? I fervently hope not, for such an overburden of past masterpieces would surely stifle the creative utterance of successive generations of artists. Any art must continually renew itself or die.

This simple fact has yet to be realized by the majority of Canadian music-lovers, to whom the word ''music'' means ''other people's music''. This is no longer the case with our national literature, nor with our painters, for example. But when we wish to hear music we tune in to German, French, Russian, English and even sometimes American, but rarely Canadian, music.

For this we can partly blame historical accident. Helmut Kallmann, in his book *A History of Music in Canada, 1534-1914,* has shown us that we have had many excellent composers in our longer-than-we-think musical history – Calixa Lavallée (our first career composer and author of ''O Canada''), Alexis Contant, Guillaume Couture, Healey Willan, Claude Champagne. But these talents were too few and far between to approach the creative ''critical mass'' which is perhaps necessary to catch creative fire in a culture.

Moreover, until fairly recently Canada did not have the performing resources to showcase its native creative talent; the Toronto Symphony Orchestra did not begin to give evening subscription concerts until the first year of the 1930's Depression and the Montreal Symphony Orchestra was not founded until 1935 (and had no good concert hall to play in until 1963). And of course their audiences had a lot of standard repertoire ''catching up'' to do.

Meanwhile in this same period a startling revolution was taking place in musical creative thought, especially in Europe. Stravinsky had begun to shred the traditional musical fabrics of writing and listening, Schönberg's ''twelve-tone'' system (in which no note or pitch is allowed sonic preference – the ultimate ''liberation'' of harmony) had knocked out the very foundations of our harmonic and key-oriented listening patterns (perhaps in a way anticipating the weightlessness of space travel?), and Varèse and others were suggesting many new avenues for fresh exploration in the name of ''music''. The modern composer had arrived.

Music has of course always had its ''modern'' composers, although by no means all composers were ''modern'' in their own time. But Monteverdi, Beethoven, Berlioz, Wagner were all greeted at first with angry incomprehension. The ''gap'', of necessity, is always with us. But the ''gap'' in twentieth-century music is undoubtedly wider than at any time in musical history (although perhaps it may be bridged more easily than we often think, with the aid of radio, recordings, tape and other modern devices).

And it was into this world that the new Canadian composer emerged, unexpected, unwanted, misunderstood, somewhat confused as to his role and intensely frustrated by the unheeding Canadian musical public and profession whose dictum on composers seemed to be "De mortuis nil nisi bonum — He's no good unless he's dead."

It was in the late 1930's that John Weinzweig wrote the first Canadian twelve-tone piece (a short movement, *Waltzling,* from a modest piano suite). At this time there were quite a few creative young men and women coming to maturity, much interested in "the new music". Their development, stifled for the six years of war, was to break out startlingly in the late forties and early fifties. Indeed by 1950 Canada could be said, for the first time in its musical history, to have a composing *fraternity,* and in their frustration they gave organizational expression to that brotherhood, the Canadian League of Composers, founded in 1951.

Basically then the problem of the new Canadian composer was, and is, a double one. Not only were, and are, his potential hearers reluctant to give him their time and attention (as are audiences with anything new and unknown), but they were and are downright hostile to the brands of "modern" music he insists on writing. Thus today's Canadian composer has *two* strikes against him.

He has several things going *for* him though. The Canadian Broadcasting Corporation, both domestic and International services, has done much to make it possible for interested listeners to hear, and even to acquire recordings of, new Canadian music.

The two performing right agencies, CAPAC (Composers, Authors and Publishers Association of Canada) and BMI Canada Limited, do much to allow composers to share in the financial rewards, where there are any, of their creative activity. The Canadian Music Centre was established in 1959 to provide practical assistance to Canadian composers, to house and catalogue their music in a central location and to promote vigorously their collected output. The Canada Council offers much support for commissions of new music and money for extra preparation and rehearsal time, not to mention that the Council specifies a "Canadian content" minimum for many performing organizations receiving its supporting grants.

Meanwhile fresh ears are growing in Canada, for the most part young ones. To children, all music is new music — Harry Somers,

Beethoven, it's all one to them; and the older young people, the "rock" generation, are probably the most sonically and musically aware of any generation its age in history, and their widening curiosity is insatiable. This is just the receptive audience the composer is waiting for and he responds to it with gusto. (Of the six composers in this book, all have taught youngsters and three have worked extensively in primary and secondary schools.) The dialogue in Canadian music may well be beginning.

Many Canadian music-lovers nowadays want to know "what is so Canadian about Canadian music?" They may be disappointed to find out that few Canadian composers really care. But did Bach care about writing "German" music, Saint-Saëns French, Elgar English, or Sibelius Finnish? Certainly their music conveys the heavy essence of national origin, but were these composers consumed with a desire to "write national"? Most certainly not! Their music just came out that way.

And so it is with Canadian composers. By and large they couldn't care less about "writing national". Indeed one, Murray Schafer, has said that the composer should "be more interested today in discovering what's going on in the world than in merely locating where one lives in it." Nationalism in music is not important to our composers. They merely want to write music which is good, challenging, and their own. The history of the creative arts assures us that our composers will inescapably, over a period of time, develop and embody certain Canadian characteristics in their work – or perhaps will embody characteristics which will afterwards be identified as "Canadian". Already certain trends in Canadian music seem to have a certain "Canadianness" – the bleak, spare line, the open, transparent (thinly-populated?) texture, the heavy seriousness (we have no "national" humour, Stephen Leacock notwithstanding).

But at this early stage Canadianness does not matter. What does matter is that our artists, our poets, our writers, our composers, should become real to us. We should feel their desire to carry on an artistic dialogue with us (in their own artistic language), and we should respond to that desire, to that language, for it is the language of our time and place, of our national community.

I know well the six composers who are the subject of this book, and I know a good deal of their music. But after having read the text of the book I must admit that I now know each and every one of them much better than I did before.

So should we all, and books such as this will help us to do so.

Office of the Executive Secretary   KEITH MACMILLAN
Canadian Music Centre, Toronto
September, 1972

PREFACE

The aim of this book is to give the reader some experience of how it feels to live as a contemporary composer in Canada. The choice of the six composers for this book was a very personal one. They are among the best, and best known in Canada, but there are certainly others who might have been included. All six are English-speaking (Quebec deserves its own volume) but are from widely different backgrounds and circumstances. I have therefore attempted to distinguish each biography by a structure and style that represents each individual's personality and music. On the whole, musical criticism is kept to a minimum.

John Weinzweig, who has provided inspiration for much of what has happened in Canadian music, is pictured at a concert of his own works as he listens with his wife, Helen. Harry Somers, Companion of the Order of Canada, burns toast and eats floorwax as a child, then embarks on an operatic odyssey. John Beckwith's creative energy is stilled for a moment in a poem set at Sharon Temple before being caught in a grid formed by *The Line Across* and *The Line Up and Down*. Norma Beecroft, CBC producer and electronic music composer, is presented, with only a few *musique concrète* distortions, as the questing romantic she really is. Zeroing in on Walter Buczynski consists of snapshots of his accomplishments and wit. Lastly, Murray Schafer's story is glossed by the echoes of his own extraordinary voice. At the end of the book is a list of the works of each composer.

Although the Canadian Music Centre is beginning a long-term project of critical monographs on Canadian composers, the secondary source materials for this book were scanty. Although much could be put together from reviews, random articles, program notes, letters, publicity releases and so forth, the bulk of the material of a personal nature came from the composers themselves through interviews and other consultations. The CBC documentary about Harry Somers produced by Norma Beecroft was an unusually helpful source. I am most appreciative of the generous way these busy people gave of their time and emotional energy.

Keith MacMillan, Executive Secretary of the Canadian Music Centre and a Director of the Canada Music Council, read the manuscript and also threw open to me the considerable re-sources of the Centre. Henry Mutsaers, Librarian of the Centre, gave continual assistance over the course of some months, making it possible for me to listen to everything of the com-posers' works that existed on Centre records or master tapes. There is nowhere else such music can be heard, since public recordings cover only a small portion of each composer's reper-toire. Scores, many in manuscript, were also made available. A note of thanks too to the other people at the Canadian Music Centre, especially Christopher Wilson.

A special thanks to Walter Buczynski, who was composer/musician-in-residence at Erindale College for the same two years as I was writer-in-residence there. My explorations in the new ways of sounding the musical deeps were encouraged by his own concerts and by those of the Canadian performers he per-suaded to give recitals at the College.

Peter Such

contents

Orpheus with his lute made trees,
And the mountain-tops that freeze,
　Bow themselves, when he did sing:
To his music plants and flowers
Ever sprung; as sun and showers
　There had made a lasting spring.

Every thing that heard him play,
Even the billows of the sea,
　Hung their heads, and then lay by.
In sweet music is such art,
Killing care and grief of heart
　Fall asleep, or hearing, die

♩ = 100

10" - - - - - - - - - - - - - - - - - -

into blow-hole

4"

5 h

sf

R.H.

5

mp   L.H.   (7) (5)   mmmmmmmmm

stagger repetitions

finger tapping
on different parts
of piano frame
for timbre contrast

john weinzweig

4"   2"

5 h   ppp

ohn Weinzweig sits with his wife Helen at a concert of *four of his works:* The Woodwind Quintet, Divertimento No. 3, Concerto for Harp and Chamber Orchestra *and* Trialogue.

He skated differently from most people – in his own style, his feet never going quite where the others expected. And so they would trip over him, slide into the boards – bang! The ref, whistling and hustling his elbow, would shove him into the penalty box. *You just watch out, Weinzweig, and don't give me any lip.* He spent more time than anybody else in that penalty box. If he'd been smaller maybe they wouldn't have been so quick to whistle him up – *but when you're big, and people are tripping all over you because you always do the unexpected, and you're making them fall flat on their faces, and they curse at you because you keep ruining their perfect schemes to score, score, win, win – well, it's no wonder, is it?*

Helen sits beside him as the string orchestra tunes up and recording technicians huddle into earphones. It's a pleasant moment for him, and there are lots of old friends in the audience to share it with. But many times before this, in the old days, the concert hall had felt like an arena where he and Helen would sit, and the thousands would be watching and listening; and the critics, with arms crossed almost as if they were gargoyles stuck up on the walls, would wait importantly, ready to turn thumbs down if they could get an excuse for it.

Sometimes a penalty box, glass barrier and all, would just seem to grow its sides around where they sat in the concert hall, in the old days; and they'd watch the game – yes, HIS GAME – being played out up there on stage, the conductor flailing his arms like a linesman eager to catch someone. . . . *Offside, ref! Offside!*

In fact there used to be concerts on the floor of the ice-rink in summertime at Varsity arena, also years ago – the Toronto Promenade Concerts, they were called. Howard Hanson, the foremost champion of American contemporary music, and at that time a director of the Eastman School of Music in Rochester, came up to conduct one time. And sitting up high in the arena, clutching his manuscript scores, watching the orchestra go at it, he, John Weinzweig, had sat, collecting his courage and waiting for the final movement to be over. The last beat. Clap clap clap. *O.K. Weinzweig, get moving quick before Hanson disappears.*

Jumping over the penalty box, over the barrier onto the rink he'd played on so often with the Harbord Collegiate Seniors, he rushed through them all, getting there even ahead of the socialites – "Mr. Hanson! Mr. Hanson!" – and waving his manuscripts. "Mr. Hanson, I wonder if you'd mind . . . ?"

But that was quite a while ago now, somewhere around 1936, and really not to be thought of – like the time after an early concert when they were at the home of one of the orchestra members. *It was a party – whoopdedo but refined – that kind, dresses down to the floor, and the host had said, "Look. I can play like Weinzweig. Want to hear?" Then he flailed his arms over the piano keys. Making this great racket with the pedal down. The party-goers thought it was really funny – oh what a scream, my dear! And laughing, laughing.*

THE WOODWIND QUINTET

> *John Weinzweig considers how this piece has influenced his composition repertoire.*

Now the players begin his *Woodwind Quintet.* This is a work written during that time he made up his mind to move away from the orchestra and compose for smaller groups of instruments. This piece was put together through 1963 and 1964. It was a way of keeping himself honest, that decision. *Chamber music, really, is the hardest discipline. You can't fake a lack of inspiration by scoring a lick or two at the cymbal in a dead spot, as you can in an orchestral work.* Up to then his whole world had been the orchestra and most of his writing was for it too, although there were occasional pieces, commissions and so on that were not. His *Sonata* for violin and piano was an early one (1941). The *Edge of The World,* 1946 – a tone poem based on Eskimo dance songs, done for the radio. That one brought forth a great batch of reviews twenty years later – in 1966! – when the Winnipeg Symphony played it on that tour through the Dakotas, Iowa, Minnesota and Wisconsin. The "Divertimento" series had begun then too, and there had been a few songs and the occasional chamber piece.

That idea of using small forces grew out of all those programmatic things he'd done in the early forties – radio writing and background music for films – work like that. Exciting at the time because his was the first original incidental music to be used on the CBC, but everything had been tied to moods and images, very visual interpretations. It was no problem writing those things. They ceased being a challenge very quickly. (Lucky he'd been steered away from going to Hollywood in 1938 when he graduated from the Eastman School of Music.) It wasn't *real* film music. He was being more or less a "sound-effects" man, filling in for the filmwriters' lack of inspiration.

This *Woodwind Quintet* grew slowly over months – all that careful planning, the decision-making over the kind of style it should be, the kind of unity he would have to give it to tie five woodwinds of different timbres together. And then the desire, in the whole thing, to make it beautiful for John Adaskin's sake, for John who'd fought so hard to let Canadian music grow on its own terms, for his friend, devoted Executive Secretary of the Canadian Music Centre, versatile musician, who died a few months before it was completed.

Nearly ten years ago he was writing the score everyone is now hearing in this concert hall – up on the second floor in the big, old house in north Toronto, on the corner of Manor Road and Servington Crescent. Old maples casting leaves at his windows. He can see – almost feel – the clusters of notes on the staves. On top the flute line whispering and whistling its own commentary, notes in its low register visiting the high territory of the clarinet, as the clarinet exchanges reedy little phrases with the soft bassoon – sonorities of those notes changing, thickening, thinning out again because of that overlap in registers. (Much later, in *Dummiyah*, an entirely different work, this time for full orchestra, he explored these changes of sounds for silence's sake.)

This particular piece, the *Woodwind Quintet,* had really grown over many years. That jazz feeling, especially in this second part where solos laze around each other in full-floating rhythms. That had been a part of his early environment – the sense of ''swing'', the sense of a rhythmic outlet for his musical ideas. Perhaps because it was the sound of his own open-hearted youth, after all, and the sound of men who had forsaken a world's fake pleasures to play their music, to breathe and to be. He'd played the saxophone himself once, as a teenager – that orchestrally exiled instrument – had even played it in dancebands, briefly, and at weddings, and once on the back of a sound-truck during an aldermanic election. (His lady lost!) The *Divertimento No. 3* with its cool, swinging bassoon he wrote in 1960 (next one on the program) and *No. 5* was done soon after – that used the trumpet and trombone. Even the *String Quartet No. 3* in 1962 with its rhythmic freedoms led to this piece. And even, maybe, from jazz jazz, came those minor seconds and thirds that this particular twelve-tone line he's now hearing is emphasizing.

The players move into this last, fast part. *Chitter-chatter, chitter-chatter, in those rapid, staccatissimo passages there's no time to think – cross-rhythms – just letting the dazzle take you away, take you away. . . .*

THE ORCHESTRA

> *John Weinzweig recalls how the orchestra played such an important part in his early life's work.*

Yes. The orchestra had been the thing. Even in his early days at Harbord Collegiate . . . an unusual school musically. Strange how that should be . . . a sudden collection of talents . . . and teacher Brian McCool making it all work. Enough to be able to command the forces to handle Gilbert and Sullivan operettas, Schubert's ''Unfinished Symphony'' and even nineteenth-century operatic overtures.

There were a lot of Jewish kids there . . . Harbord being in that area at that time. Other immigrants are in the district now. Most of the successful Jewish people having moved up, out and away . . . from those roots . . . in the tribal clusters of stores and houses and square, tiny, balconied synagogues, some of them underground theatres now . . . that's good! Here and there, still, the kosher star sign left unremoved under an old store's awning. In rooming houses, mezuzahs painted eight times over are still stuck forever on old door moldings, still carrying their messages of peace, wisdom, blessing.

There were many good violinists. He himself played the mandolin, receiving those intense lessons at his parochial school, the Workmen's Circle Peretz School. It was named for the Jewish-Polish poet, and its classes welcomed children of workers who had broken from the Orthodox ways.

And many times at Harbord Collegiate he'd had the chance to conduct rehearsals, and even performances at assemblies. That's what he'd wanted to be – a conductor – at first. His bright, anxious, beautiful mother (too much imagination for her time) wanted her children to get all the education they could. Music was important; so, at fourteen – before it was too late – he got started. With piano lessons. But his fingers couldn't stay with Czerny. They wandered off on their own.

In the next five years he played many other instruments. *What you couldn't do with them!* Filling in for a member of the orchestra who had graduated, he played the double-bass. (At first with only three strings, later with four.) Previously, after one lesson from its original manipulator, he blew the sousaphone. After that came the tenor sax, and all the while there was that piano keyboard and his fingers roaming further afield. Meanwhile his brother Morris was developing into a professional saxophonist and clarinetist. Morris had started at twelve on the piano when his mother had decided both he and John should start lessons at once.

It was 1929 when he turned sixteen. The Depression hit hard in the College Street area. His father had become a manufacturer by then, a partner in Weinzweig and Perenson, who manufactured fur coats in the Commodore Building near Spadina and barely managed to survive when customers owing them money went bankrupt. Because of this John later took an accounting

8   soundprints

course – so that he'd be able to help the firm out.

His father had come over from Poland in 1907. What must it have been like spending time in jail in Poland because of his involvement in socialist and union movements? And then being granted amnesty in an erratic moment or two of political expediency (Poland was under Russian control at that time). *Lucky he'd been given that tip to get out while the getting was still good. . . .*

Once in Toronto his father had run into others who were in similar circumstances. *Amazing coincidence.* This beautiful, temperamental girl from his home town in Poland he'd always wished to know better! It hadn't taken long for them to get married.

To survive, his father blocked men's hats, became a fur cutter in the garment district, worked making fur gloves. At one point, he worked for Eaton's; another time, he headed for New York, worked hard, came back with his skills, and opened his own store on College Street. Later, even though by then a capitalist manufacturer, he still sent John and Morris to the left-wing Peretz School. That was the kind of thing he'd do.

John Weinzweig remembers the small, dedicated school. He remembers that summer session at its camp near Pickering, Ontario, when there was that double electrocution in New York. 1927. The Sacco-Vanzetti case. The whole camp sent a telegram of protest. John's friends from that time seemed to get involved in politics or in social concerns. But not him. . . . *My son a composer? Well. If that's what he wants to be. . . .* He'd never campaigned politically or anything like that. It was possible, though, the school might have influenced the way he acted when he felt something important needed to be done in the music world. Waiting right now for his *Divertimento No. 3* to start reminds him that the Canadian League of Composers, for instance, was his doing.

John Weinzweig and his family were then living in a tiny bungalow. Coming back to Toronto from Ottawa where he'd been stationed with the RCAF they'd found it impossible to rent. Poor Helen, heavy with Daniel, had searched with John, dragging Paul behind. Children. Landlords didn't want children. ''We should buy a home, John." But what if they couldn't manage the mortgage? *It's different now; but then . . . being an artist . . . you were scared . . . naturally . . . of a long-term commitment like that.* But it had worked out fine although it was touch-and-go now and then. *Hadn't it always been that way? . . . That was the price you paid for being what you wanted to be.*

Harry Somers arrived at the house first. He'd just got back from France. (This was 1951.) Then Sam Dolin arrived. Both of them were ex-pupils he'd introduced to new composition techniques. Aaron Copland had warned them about what had happened to an American organization similar to the one they were proposing to set up in Canada. It had included Darius Milhaud and other European greats among its members. Collapse had come because, among other things, it was a body far too large and amorphous for meaningful contact, and it had tipped over under its own weight. To survive, it had merged with the International Society for Contemporary Music.

Harry Somers and Sam Dolin wanted to know how you could keep an organization small with a realistic base, without being elitist about it. A tough question. And there were all those competent church organists who dabbled with their own arrangements of this and that – all very pleasing and enjoyable to their congregations and their church choirs – but should they be considered composers? The solution had been to have prospective members submit a lengthy, serious piece of work, preferably orchestral, which a committee would review. The result was an organization which grew to a membership of almost sixty by the time of its twenty-first birthday in 1972. This base was large enough to foster interest in extending the work of Canadian composers yet small enough to maintain liaison with its members.

Helen came in at the end of the discussion. In the tiny room they drank to the success of the new organization. To celebrate, Helen produced a fresh-baked cherry pie. As founder (and eventually, the following year, its first president) he, John Weinzweig, cut the first slice – waving the knife like a conductor's baton. The Canadian League of Composers was born. . . . The following May, to mark the event, a surprise celebration – a concert of

Weinzweig's music – was arranged by Somers, Adaskin, and other friends and former pupils.

What was it about being a conductor that had attracted him? Was it his sense of the dramatic? Or was he drawn by the power of the orchestra? *A huge instrument . . . an amazing artistic tool . . . capable of producing any variety of sound you wanted it to.*

After Harbord Collegiate there had been no orchestra to conduct. For two years he had missed it, struggling instead to pass the business course at Central Technical School so he could help out in his father's company as a bookkeeper and typist. Taking private lessons in piano and conducting with Reginald Stewart he would come home from work, put time into his courses, and practise. It didn't show, then, because he told nobody, but he was already writing music. It was very romantic, and conventional. . . . Once the extramural music course (which grew into the music faculty) began operating at the University of Toronto, he'd signed up for it, since by then he was considered a senior member of the Royal Conservatory of Music student body. Besides, it was cheaper, at fifty dollars for registration, than taking lessons privately. Sir Ernest MacMillan was the Dean – and Healey Willan was associated with it as well.

All that student talent was going to waste. It just needed someone to get it together. Why not he, John Weinzweig, as that someone? Maybe the Peretz philosophy had influenced him without his really being aware of it. Maybe. Using his music review column in *The Varsity*, the University of Toronto student newspaper, for publicity, he soon got an orchestra together. The University of Toronto Symphony Orchestra. The problem of getting scores was partially solved by borrowing from Harbord Collegiate, his old Alma Mater. Brian McCool, later made Head of the Music Education division in the Ontario Department of Education, was happy to help out. The Faculty of Music didn't offer as much support as might have been expected. But the Students' Administrative Council was eventually persuaded to give funds, and somehow the orchestra managed to hold together for its first three years, long enough for it to become an institution in its own right.

The League. The Orchestra. Then later there was the Canadian Music Centre. He helped formulate the original concept and obtain support from the Canada Council in 1959. Being a director of the board as he is can keep a person busy. Especially since he's also vice-president of CAPAC, the Composers, Authors and Publishers Association of Canada. And besides that there's his unremitting battle with the music publishers and symphony orchestras. "In the area of publication and recording, Canada continues to hold the status of an emerging nation," he's fond of letting them know.

So, if you've always been independent, always made your own way, and you run into an injustice here, or a need for something there, and you happen to feel you can do something about it – well – that's a kind of citizenship – you don't have to be a regular politician. He had always tried to make his point in the way he knew best, as he did in 1960 with *Wine of Peace* (a plea for sanity and tolerance) at the International Conference of Composers in Stratford, which he chaired; and also, ten years later, with *Dummiyah* (Silence). In this piece, returning to the orchestra again, he was able to speak, at last, of the Nazi atrocities through a death-hush of muted orchestral forces. . . .

DIVERTIMENTO NO. 3

> *(John Weinzweig's wife, Helen, is reminded of other times and other places. . . .)*

Helen unfolds her program after the applause for the *Woodwind Quintet.* She looks over the *Divertimento No. 3* program notes: *Commissioned for the Saskatoon Symphony Orchestra. Reflects the jazz outlook in its phrasing, structure and rhythmic fluidity. It is organized in the serial technique with rhythmic figures favourable to the swing manner.*

She's heard every première of John's works. *Proud . . . of him, of course.* John always turning to her first – *How was it, Helen?* She knowing his confidence in himself to be unshakable by praise or blame – praise especially. He always knows . . . *what's wrong, what's not quite there . . .* and sometimes she has told

12 soundprints

him so, listening over the years as his pieces grew . . . like branches, twigs, in changed seasons, sometimes growing much too stark, too cold for her passionate tastes but rooted always . . . *rooted . . . by his deep integrity. Especially those years when with a monk's fervour he would strip all ornament, all glad excess away . . . keep only absolute essentials and no more . . . so tight . . . cryptic . . . puritan!* He was testing his art. As composer and critic Udo Kasemets wrote about that time, ''For a dozen years he forced a rigid discipline on himself, keeping his expressive means in tight bonds and controlling sternly his own process of maturing.''

And what a different thing this *Divertimento* for solo bassoon is from the piece played at that first Toronto première (which she nearly missed). He'd written that one, *The Enchanted Hill,* as his graduation composition from Eastman, for his Master's degree. He'd been the first Canadian to go there after graduating from the new course at the University of Toronto. What he'd learned at the Toronto Faculty of Music was more theoretical than creative. He'd been taking Harmony with Leo Smith, Orchestration with Sir Ernest MacMillan, and Conducting with Reginald Stewart. It was not a music school directed to composition at all (although he took Counterpoint with Healey Willan). But Healey Willan, who later was made Companion of the Order of Canada, was a British organist, steeped in those British traditions. A very successful composer, but as a teacher he had more interest in imparting technique than in developing innovation. *Going to Eastman? To America? Definitely not the thing to do, my boy!*

Howard Hanson, composer, Director of the Eastman School of Music, and pioneer in encouraging American composition, had been impressed by John. Perhaps because John had had the nerve, the year before, to press his manuscripts upon him. *Yes! When you graduate, John, why don't you come to us?* That was the first real encouragement to John Weinzweig's creative hopes. And Hanson later would conduct the first performance of John's Composition Thesis when he eventually obtained his postgraduate degree.

Those first six weeks at Eastman were lonely for John. He shared an apartment with an elderly couple. He'd written to Helen about those weeks. *How it felt to be entirely cut off in strange circumstances. What it meant to realize you had committed yourself to a life that only a very few approved of, and a life which offered nothing but material insecurity, and only the vaguest promise of, even, artistic success at the end of a long haul.*

He and she had known each other, to say hello, since childhood, and had even gone to the same school. But their families had grown their different ways. They'd never gone out together before that happened. Helen, herself, living with her mother who was ostracized because she was separated from her legal husband, had been single-minded, clever, ambitious. At nineteen Helen was head of a brokerage house. Because of her mixed-up family life she had developed a deep survival ability, a capacity to adjust, which she'd converted into her success.

At seventeen she had had to act with unusual strength when her mother had sent her to Milan to visit her father. As part of the war-game her parents sporadically conducted, she was virtually imprisoned there, her father destroying her passport and attempting to keep her in paternal bondage in Italy. Finally she had had to go to the police and run a gamut of bureaucracies before getting safely back to Canada.

Her material success as a stockbroker was well thought of because that was the ambition everyone had for children in those Depression days of the thirties. But suddenly, with an attack of tuberculosis, she'd turned from all that, spent two years poring over every book she could get her hands on, and had discovered a totally different world of emotion and sensibility.

Running into John, going to concerts with him, she'd found a person with similar notions – a person who wanted to be an artist, an intellectual, who wanted to give to the world rather than take from it. At this time his lovely mother had finally broken down and gone to live in her vivid imagination. Her sickness, her loss when he was still only a teenager of eighteen, was a painful experience – and a worse one for his younger sister. . . .

Strange how she, Helen, and John had both grown up. Was this the same John who had swung the bat as one of the "Young Maccabees", standing there spitting on his hands in the raucous ballpark, being urged on by their Anglo-Saxon mentor Alan Coatsworth? And was she the tense, vivid, pragmatic, young College Street kid who had quietly kept ears and eyes open to see where her advantage might be?

Soon after John's graduation from Eastman they were married. It was 1940. The War had begun. For years John never knew it but her mother helped pay the rent, which he had no idea was a few dollars higher than Helen had told him. He'd been supported slenderly at Eastman by his father and his own accumulated savings. Now, without these resources, he was attempting to build up a clientele of composition students at the Conservatory and to pick up whatever odd jobs were available for a postgraduate in music.

It wouldn't have been so difficult if, while in his graduating year at Eastman, 1938, John hadn't one day idly played a new acquisition to the record library, *The Lyric Suite,* a string quartet by Alban Berg, who had died just a few years previously in 1935. What he heard excited him more than any one piece ever had. It was his introduction to the twelve-tone method of Schoenberg. But it was a composing technique no one was able to explain to him. Even in the United States this method, first written about in the early 1920's, was regarded with deep suspicion.

Hanson had been unsympathetic. Once a year a concert was held at which were played works by recent graduates of the school. Along with all the others of his year, Weinzweig submitted works completed the season following their graduation. His works, however, bore unmistakable twelve-tone influences. They were cordially rejected.

As early as 1939 his compositions began to move rapidly away from the Strauss and Berlioz influences of his youth. Being known as a "twelve-tone man" was a lonely life. Everyone else at the Conservatory, or otherwise connected with music, he had told Helen, "suspects I'm plotting the downfall of Bach." Reac-

john weinzweig 15

tion to him was violent. It was like being accused of being a fifth columnist.

The Enchanted Hill, then, was one of his last programmatic works written in a more ''conventional'' mode. It was given its Toronto première in 1943. That was the piece she almost missed.

John had been nervous. He wore his best suit. She, herself, was dressed and packed. *You know, John, I think it's starting.* He looked at her swollen belly. They'd suspected it might be tonight. *There are the workings of fate for you. O.K. I'll call Dr Cohen.* Dr Benjamin Cohen was the physician in whose office Helen had worked as a secretary since marrying John. (When her office friends had found out she was married one had said, *What does he do? He's a composer,* she'd replied. *Yeah. But what does he do?)*

At the hospital the contractions started coming closer together. *I'm going to miss it. I'm going to miss your première.* John: *I'm not going either.* She: *You've got to go. What can you do hanging around here?* He: *All right. I'll come back right after.* He'd charged off into the night. Benjamin Cohen had an idea. He raced around the wards until he found a radio. He persuaded the owner to lend it to him for the night. He came back to Helen. *How's it going?*

Hanging on to the bedrails, she was catching her breath between spasms. *O.K. They're coming faster now.* Dr Cohen: *I got something for you. There. We can plug it in over here.* A radio. Of course.

She'd hear it after all. She closed her eyes. *Tonight you are going to hear the Toronto Symphony Orchestra giving a world première performance of* The Enchanted Hill, *a work based on the poetry of Walter de la Mare and written by the young Canadian composer John Weinzweig. . . .*

So she didn't miss it. Later that night when John had come back happy to see her after all the applause, she'd been able to tell him and share his elation. Then something with a few million years of practice had begun conducting her body. Her mind, handing over its control, became merely one instrument in the whole orchestration until it ended with a sharp cry . . . Paul . . . flushing pink . . . with his first breaths . . . taking on real life . . . beside her . . . his delicate perfect hands. . . .

Harry Somers had done a short documentary on John for the CBC. During the interview John had told Harry what the "Divertimento" series meant to him. They were (as in traditional music) light musical pieces rather than dramatic ones, with an outward-looking emotionality; works that were not afraid to be witty. Yet they were serious — serious music doesn't always mean tragic music — and always reflected his thinking in a general way. Especially was that so in the slow movements, which were usually their strongest portions and which probed their lyric intensity.

The first of this series, for flute and strings, later recorded with Victor Feldbrill conducting and Gordon Day playing the flute, was written in 1945. It won the Olympic Competition for Chamber Music in 1948, one of the last times the Olympics included a musical contest. Udo Kasemets thought John's first two *Divertimenti,* along with *Interlude in an Artist's Life,* the *Piano Sonata* and the second *String Quartet,* were part of the crystallizing of his serial techniques — a process which had led to their "ascetic clarity" and "brittleness".

But as Kasemets had also pointed out, John Weinzweig's dedication to serialism wasn't in any way imitative. Just as his fingers had strayed from Czerny into his own improvisations, John had early realized he had to interpret the "row" in his own way. Kasemets had mentioned this in his essay about John written in 1960 for the *Canadian Music Journal:* ". . . he had to seek for different treatment of the row from Schoenberg and the Viennese school. Instead of basing his serial constructions on Schoenberg's ideal . . . Weinzweig regarded the baroque principle of total unity of a single movement as his model. For him the twelve-note series is not a unifying element for all movements of the work. He rather emphasizes the contrast of individual movements by basing them on different rows." Yes. What kept John's compositions together wasn't the new atonal principle but the overall emotional effect. The "row" principle was his way of working it out; not a thing used for its own sake.

But by this third *Divertimento* – the one they are now hearing – John had begun picking up on those rhythmic elements from jazz, those swing inflections. It was finished in 1960, in the early part of the year, in winter. Against the Neoclassic coolness of earlier works it danced like the fire in the living room of their new house at Manor Road and Servington Crescent.

In their first, smaller house Helen would absorb the phrases and processes of compositions as John would build them up on the piano. Later she would hear them, remember them, and associate them with washing diapers or doing dishes. Only once had she commented to him on his music while it was in process. He'd been exploring the same phrases over and over. *For God's sake, stop doing that intellectual crap and let yourself go!*

Afterwards she was ashamed. But John always tells everyone how highly developed her musical intelligence is. He respects her judgement although confident in his own. She is a good critic. The first member of his audience. And at the end of this *Divertimento* he will turn his head in the white noise of the applause and ask, *How was it, Helen?*

He'd told Harry Somers in the interview, "There's no point in writing music for myself. If there was I'd just write for the piano so I could play it myself. You must be thinking of an audience as soon as you get to doing things for an orchestra, thinking of a response. Those who deny it are defending themselves from criticism. There's no point in writing unless it has a social purpose."

In addition to the swing inflections in the whole piece, John had explored the nature of the bassoon itself. Traditionally it had two roles: either a clown or a tragedian. In this piece he wanted to turn it into an extrovert solo instrument in its own right with its own peculiar sonorities.

This concentration on the capacities of various instruments has always been one of John's fascinations. It's part of his philosophy of considering the style of a piece, and the capabilities of the medium he is going to use, before he writes a note. Another *Divertimento,* the fourth (which was actually completed in 1968 AFTER *No. 5),* forced the clarinet soloist James Morton to de-

18   soundprints

velop a new technique, in which sustained notes ride over and through the strings' patterns like wavering sirens, whose sonorities become lost in the string sounds, then reveal themselves as the string notes decay. Sometimes the tones are like those made by blowing in a bottle, sounds induced without the use of reeds. In addition, unlike most clarinet pieces, the first movement is tremendously percussive with high sustained notes – a sharp contrast to the random events of the mid-portion and the rhythmic ''swing'' motifs of the relaxed ending. An exciting piece for the clarinetist to display his virtuosity.

Commission requirements pick my field of battle. (John's fond of catchy images like that: *Those Englishmen you know, most of them haven't marched up to the Berg Line yet.* Or. *Yes. I heard the* Lyric Suite *by Alban Berg and it knocked me for a row.* And. *Oh. I've been out all morning doing some rowing.)*

The *Divertimenti* aren't long pieces. A few years ago, modern works used to be played merely as novelties. If a piece were short it had a much greater chance of inclusion in a program because it wouldn't be long enough to tax the audience. Ten minutes was a long piece of work. Five minutes was the preferred length.

This *Divertimento No. 3* is into its final leg already. The phrases are familiar to Helen. Although it is serially constructed and atonal, John has made no rigid attempt to avoid *tonal centres.* That, too, is part of his different treatment of the twelve-tone system. Most adherents carefully avoid such accidents; but they are led instead into awkward manipulations purely for that reason. To John, sounding the beauties of another convention adds an extra dimension to his audience's response while he is still maintaining the integrity of his basic mode.

In fact, John has used his serial mode deliberately in ways which sometimes include old conventions and traditions. He enjoys that. That's why it gave him a lift to come up with the idea of the minor seconds and thirds in the tone-row of the *Woodwind Quintet* so that they would suggest the sound of jazz. Also, in the work called *Wine of Peace,* he did a similar thing with two poems (which seemed to go so well together) that he'd found in an anthology. *Life is a Dream* by de la Barca; and an anonymous Arabian poem, *City of Brass. They've both got common Moorish roots, Helen.*

He'd come up with the notion of using a common Eastern musical fragment, $E^\flat$ D $B^\flat$, and integrating it into the tone-rows that formed the basis of the two dramatic songs. *Save up your soul and taste / the beautiful Wine of Peace.* He'd dedicated it to the United Nations ''where the dreams of Mankind can become a reality.'' The piece includes his first important alto saxophone part, which is usually played by his brother, Morris.

Much earlier, in 1949, he'd been given a commission for a ballet. He'd been influenced by Aaron Copland's approach, and had tried to integrate Indian and French folk-song elements in the score, in a clean treatment which tried to let these naïve, often pentatonic, melodies create the piece's style – rather than having it forced on them. The Barn Dance segment is performed frequently because of its great vitality and rhythm. The piece was based on and took its name from an Iroquois folk-myth which the French Canadians had picked up; it was entitled *Red Ear of Corn.*

That title caused a few crazy laughs! John hadn't wanted to be associated with anything suggesting ''corn''. But it was the ''red'' part that caused the trouble. *It was the time of the ''Red Scare'' and poor old Dad, applying for that visa . . . to cross the border . . . actually got questioned about it by the American Consul!*

And now Helen turns to him. It's already *Intermission,* as her program says.

John rises. People crowd around him. She stands too. She comes up to his chest. His arm naturally surrounds her shoulder; hers around his firm waist. *That's, Vic Tanny's Health Club for you.* She hugs him. He's glad of the audience's enjoyment.

The grey in his hair and in his mustache softens the sharp, witty Marx brothers look he used to have when he was younger. Now his natural warmth and seriousness come through more easily to people at first meeting. Large glasses, too, make his eyes the focus of his face.

20 soundprints

Will she write about him one day? Maybe if her writing gift that bloomed so late keeps growing she will be able to do so. Her novelist's sensibility makes her conscious of her own appearance beside him now. Low key. In the things she wears she feels close to the young people she knows. *Nothing brittle or glaring. Soft textures. Warm deep colours.*

John is describing how he is at work on a new *Divertimento,* the sixth, which he is readying for the Third World Saxophone Congress, being held in Toronto. He's using a soloist as he writes it so that he can hear directly the effects he wants to achieve.

Someone asks, *Isn't that more or less the way you approached the Harp Concerto we're going to hear next?* Yes. But that was a different thing again, since he actually took lessons on the harp to discover its potentialities before he wrote a note.

Lights dim. On stage, the harpist tilts back her stately classic instrument. On its pedestal it rests in perfect balance by her shoulder, leaning on her lightly, giving up its proud stance, for the moment, to a beautiful and clever woman . . . *Helen* . . . *There's a name to carry with you all your life!*

CONCERTO FOR HARP AND CHAMBER ORCHESTRA

> *(John Weinzweig remembers the unusual circumstances and problems of this commission.)*

His hand sliding down the rail, his feet descending scales of stone steps into the basement, sub-basement, of the Edward Johnson Building, three floors below his office — he was looking for the harp he knew was down there waiting somewhere. Who had played it last, when? Harp, heavenly instrument — but his feet beating rhythm were taking him like Orpheus into the underworld (at the end of each flight stop: one two turn and go down again) — one of the most ancient instruments, adjusting itself through the ages, its octave first five-toned, then seven, and finally chromaticized, still clumsily perhaps; feet on seven pedals, hands on seven strings, little brass discs clinging as it sings. But he would soon find out.

Thing about the harp is its tone. Its high-coloured tone (as with most mediaeval instruments) and its capacity for resonance – those marvellous guitaric, brassy, tympanic sounds – strange timbres. And wasn't that what he was growing more interested in?

The eighteenth century's studied harmonies had relegated the harp to obscurity until the great technician Sebastien Erard in 1810 added the double pedal action and the double discs to sharpen each string, so that Debussy, great composer, could rescue it with the right kind of music, and later Carlos Salzedo, celebrated instrumentalist, could extend its range of technique and colour during the early years of this century.

That harp. It was buried in the vaults down there somewhere.

Judy Loman had said, *If you can get to a harp we'll make this a real collaboration, John. I'll tutor you in the fundamentals so you'll know what it can do.* She herself had been a pupil of Salzedo, and the Toronto Repertory Ensemble and Judy Loman wanted to commission a work that would tax all her skills. It was a Centennial Year project of the Canadian Music Centre.

John had accepted the task. What a difference, though, from what he'd been doing – just having completed that piano concerto in the early spring, and now having to reorient from a twelve-tone keyboard to a seven-tone pedal system that needed both hands and feet!

He'd found it. It was in a dark vault of a room. He turned the lights on. The room was close to the electronic music studio. He walked around it, studying the logic of the harp's heavy, graceful construction.

The soundbox, or body – with its sounding-board belly of a paler colour – was wide at the base and narrowed over his shoulder. The harp's neck curved like a swan's away from him. That curve, strangely, made it easier for his eyes to stay in focus than a straight edge would have. The massive forepillar, like a Greek column, rested on the pedal box. The pedal's mechanisms were hidden in there, then ran up the hollow column and along the neck to spin the double rows of brass discs which shortened the strings a semitone or a whole tone.

Experimenting, he realized it was tuned in C flat. Thus, pushing the C pedal one notch down brought it to C, and pushing two notches down brought it to C sharp. There was one pedal for each of seven notes in the 6½ octaves – a marvellous range – and the bound wire strings of the bass sounded with a different colour from the gut strings higher up.

Getting lessons from Judy in the fundamentals he'd spent the fall working on that practice harp. By September 1966 he felt himself ready to begin the formal organization of the piece. He would use the instrumental forces of a string quintet or string orchestra, and a woodwind quintet. He'd fuse the harp's range of many colours with pointillistic, percussive gestures to give it a dramatic role, rather than the ornamental role to which it had been relegated. Also he would have to bend its essentially diatonic limitations into a twelve-tone style. His concerto would consist of six interconnected sections, and the twelve-tone row would be elaborated by the harp's twelve different colourations, climaxed by a set of five harp cadenzas which would reflect short, introductory solos by flute, oboe, clarinet, horn and bassoon. The string quintet would previously have been used in the opening sections to create muted sound cushions on which the harp's sharp, percussive, opening tones would be presented like sparkling diamonds.

For once, the première (April 30, 1967) was an unqualified success. Judy Loman gave a beautiful performance. *The Toronto Telegram's* Kenneth Winters commented: ''. . . so admirable in itself and so admirably performed . . . a work of some loveliness and considerable fascination. Technically adroit, intellectually resilient, musically comely, it offers serious but attractive challenges to both players and audience and is clearly intended for permanent use by both. . . . It works, it makes sense, and I think it will last.'' And John Kraglund of *The Globe and Mail* wrote: ''The principal aim of the work seems to be the exploitation of the technical and tonal range of the harp, an aim in which the composer has been quite successful. The success could be attributed in this instance not only to the virtuosity of Miss Loman, but also to Weinzweig's employment of the other instrumental sonorities to set off rather than to obscure the solo part.''

As he hears it now, John Weinzweig wonders whether, if he could do it again, he might change anything in that piece. *No. You mustn't get into that revision thing.* Besides, this Harp Concerto was really the culmination of a certain period in his art. His later commissions had, in fact, defied the nature of the radio medium and had been working towards a dramatic texture through considerations of the stage. And following this, his next big work, *Dummiyah* (composed between January and April 1969), had explored drama, timbre and colour more than line — just as his sixth *Divertimento,* still in the works, was liberating his previous conception of ''swing''.

SILENCE

(John Weinzweig sits ''under the volcano''.)

Now, in the warm summer silence as the soprano, flautist and pianist take their places for *Trialogue,* next on the program and his most recent piece, he is reminded of *Dummiyah* (Silence) again. He'd put it together during four months in a ''casa'' in the hot Mexico sun right under the stunning mute volcano of Popocatepetl in Cuernavaca. Two things had coincided to make it possible: a sabbatical leave from his teaching post at the Faculty of Music and a Canada Council senior arts award.

The Mexican interior . . . a God-forsaken land . . . poor people there have to make do with the dregs of the world's natural resources . . . brittle and stony . . . with cactus hands beseeching some small hint of mercy from a relentless sky.

Since 1967 and the Harp Concerto, travelling, too, has been part of the new phase in his life. Except for his time at the Eastman School in Rochester he had pretty well stayed in Canada. In 1967, right after the Harp Concerto, he'd gone to Europe, to Britain, to Edinburgh for the Festival there. In Edinburgh, William Wordsworth, composer, simple-living man, descendant of the famous poet, had walked them up several lush hills and walked them down again. It felt as if they were in an old, green

24   soundprints

nursery rhyme. What a change Mexico was after that!

The vast stillness of that volcano confronted him, in Mexico, every morning. He used the rented piano very little. It was more in keeping with the nature of *Dummiyah* for him to stand outside with a sheet of music paper on a stand and conduct, looking across the blue mountain ridges to Popo's white cap with its thin plume of smoke, and to try to find the secret of rhythm (in silence). *To use the orchestra like a silent volcano – that was the solution – to use it as a mass that hardly moves and has little energy.*

At night, reading about the Eichmann trial in Jerusalem, he sat numbed by the evidence given by survivors of the Nazi brutalities. By day he fashioned those repressed emotions into a creative, emotional intensity. Near the end of four months the piece was finished. The hot season began almost at once, and the day after *Dummiyah* was completed the volcano was obscured by a persistent cloud haze. He looked for it every day. But it was gone. He never saw it again.

Dummiyah began with silence. Victor Feldbrill, conducting the première, moved his baton for several bars before the orchestra made its first, tentative sound. Talking to June Graham about it for an article in the CBC *Times*, Weinzweig said: ''I wanted to handle it in a subtle way and avoid obvious devices for creating a romantic concept, such as hitting the audience over the head with an orchestral explosion. There isn't a single *fortissimo* in the whole work. Its one movement is seventeen minutes long. As I've said, it opens with several bars of silence so the audience is already involved, although no sound is audible. And the last thirty seconds are conducted silence. The players are still in playing position, because the piece isn't over when they stop playing. Psychologically the last sound is retained. The only time the full orchestra is used is for four very soft bars at the end – a different concept of *tutti*. I knew how I would handle the orchestra. Then I developed it from abstract concept to dramatic concept – silence as the unspeakable horror of the Nazi holocaust. The only reaction to it is silence. . . .''

> *(Helen senses the audience's response to the artistic risks of this piece.)*

It's a gamble. An artistic gamble. Helen is thinking about John's latest commissions. But also about her own novel-writing. As, in her own writing, she is trying to make the whole scene ring psychologically true by risky plunges into waters that sink underground, that penetrate the dark unconscious (of herself as well as her characters?), so John is into another exploratory phase that involves more of himself, perhaps, than he has dared ever show before. As a beginner no one expects much from her; they are pleased by her unsuspected talent. *But what if, like John, you've been expected to keep surpassing yourself all these years? What kind of risks need you take then?*

Trialogue concerns the interplay between three dramatic musical forces: the piano, the flute, and the vocalist. They've got themselves arranged, now, the vocalist impressive in her long gown, the pianist in the middle (more or less), the flautist on the other side. It begins with ''Sh, never'', a phrase which, half-sung, half-spoken, half-chanted, explores and fragments the phonetic properties of language. The piano and flute chime into the vocal patterns as the piece moves through the short sections one by one. Occasionally the vocalist strokes glissandi on the piano-strings. John had written the score so that the sections could be performed in any order, but the trio are taking no chances and are doing it ''straight''. ''Jump Cow'', ''Cry, Sigh, Why'', ''My dear, etcetera''. The audience gets a laugh out of that one. It's a humorous section dealing with the hypocritical rhetoric of a love letter (or is it?). ''Wow!'' ''Who Said?'' ''Do I?'' ''Oh, that I were'', ''Listen'', ''Hear Me'', ''Oh, my'', ''All is still'', ''Yes, No'', ''Sh''.

Well. The audience aren't too sure about that one. She can sense what they are thinking. *Yes. It's enjoyable. It's very clever. There are some good sounds in it. Yes. It's called a stagepiece. Look. Right there in the program notes. Is it music? Is it valid? He's never done anything like that before. I mean, you expect*

26   soundprints

that sort of thing from somebody like. . . .

Then the audience re-read their program notes (John always bothers to write those himself): . . . *the free association of ideas . . . explores states of feeling from reflect to reflex in a sequence of random moments . . . inner monologue of the singer . . . burst flashes of memory, fantasy and reality . . . flute and piano in a three-way dialogue of total involvement . . . found, heard, quote, unquote, absurd, overheard . . . pass the plate, and it came to pass . . . a sound has no legs to stand on. . . .*

But people do have legs and suddenly they are standing and clapping. Handshakes, handshakes, smiles, smiles. *What did you mean, Mr Weinzweig, by . . . ? I found it a little. . . . In that fast section. . . . Especially on those high. . . .*

AFTERTONES

(Art grows in solitude.)

They squeeze out. It was an early concert. There's light still in the summer sky. Because of the concert John has an inspiration he wants to work out for his latest *Divertimento*. For her, there's that chapter to finish revising. *Getting down to it is really all it takes.* They squeeze hands, kiss and separate.

Helen wanders west to her studio. It's a small, front room over an artshop on Markham Street near Honest Ed's. Her friends tease her about it. But they don't realize her roots are there. And when she goes there to write, it all seems to come together more easily. She wants to rediscover her roots, her past, so that she can grow as an artist herself. John, on his way to their sedate home, doesn't need that. *He's beyond that. Like the strong aftertones of a cymbal, his art is widening out, out, with the years. . . .*

John turns the key. The house is empty. Paul and Danny grew up long ago. *It's nice to see them when they drop in. They do it often.* His boys. He pours a brandy and soda and sits a minute in the living room. It's the kind of room filled with pieces of furniture of different styles that look as though they've been collected over ages. The truth is, Helen and he ran into a store and ordered the whole lot in half an hour. *Why mess around? If you like something about every style it means there's always a piece someone else will like.*

He sinks into one of two high, wing-back chairs done in velvet. His feet rest on the matching shag rug. He puts his drink on a brass-foil coffee table. Under an abstract across from him is an eighteenth-century console. Behind him is the fireplace with another abstract over the mantlepiece. Beside him is a chrome and black-leather Barcelona chair. At the far end is an Italian Modern steel, chrome and glass side-table. The other decorations on the walls are an Indian stone-rubbing and an enormous painting of a lightbulb by Norman White, the electronic sculptor. He fiddles with a set of interlocking plastic cubes — mulling over his inspiration. *Yes. In the last little while things have been easier. Ever since becoming a member of the Music Faculty in 1952, in fact. Teaching. Yes.* If it hadn't been for the talents who had come to him he'd have given it up long ago. But those students always made him learn too, as he kept watching them grope (as he once had to) and seeing them eventually find their own clear way of doing what they had to do. And many had become excellent composers themselves, creating in just a couple of decades a really fine society of musicians and composers. *This country is well on its way. . . .*

Last winter had seemed short, with that flying visit to Mexico again. That was the first time he'd sought the winter sun. They'd stayed on the coast, this time, in Zihuatanejo, where a lot of Canadians seem to wind up for some reason. He'd gone fishing for the experience of it. What a joke that turned out to be. Trolling with bait, he'd got a bite. *Quick! Reel it in!* But it wasn't a fish at all. It was a bird! It had swallowed the bait. *Greedy. Look what that cost it.* They'd had to knock it unconscious and struggle to take the hook out of its mouth. Then they'd put it over the side to rest on the waves. It would be all right, when it came to. It would stretch and fly again, oblivious perhaps to who had caught it or what had happened. . . . Why did it happen that everything he, John Weinzweig, did, he had to do it differently?

"Timbres." *Darn it.* He'd have to get that tape down to the Music Centre. The title had been changed to *Around the Stage in Twenty-Five Minutes During Which a Variety of Instruments Are Struck!* He liked that better than "Timbres". It was commissioned by the CBC in 1971 for William Cahn, the percussionist. He'd tried out every conceivable percussion instrument while he was writing it to make sure it came out sounding right. . . .

He reaches his study. The latest of his *Divertimenti* waits for him to finish. It's for saxophone and strings. In this piece he has already further developed and liberated his previous notions of "swing" and gone further than ever with jazz rhythms. He has also added many elements of controlled improvisation – something he'd begun with *Trialogue.*

He strolls up and down for a few minutes, thinking. There's a new addition to his study. He finally got it sent up from New York. *What an extravagance!* A large Turkish cymbal – a thin one – the faint rings, where the brass has been turned, expand like ripples in water and fall off its fine edge into untuned space.

Ching! He hits it with his fingernail again. It will ring for minutes. Where does its pure sound disappear to? His study fills with it – *like sounding brass . . . and the walls of Jericho . . . fell down.* When seemingly the plate's last soundtrace finds its way out of his study windows, he bends low over the cymbal.

Hear it? A steady, very low hum . . . an aftertone of tremendous but muted energy. Last night, breathing close every few minutes, he had timed the aftertone's duration for nearly half an hour. *You have to get to know your instruments. You really have to get to know them. . . .*

harry somers

Sometimes he slept during the day to make up for it. Judging when his parents were properly asleep was the hardest part. And in winter it meant having to smuggle his heavy coat into the bedroom so that he wouldn't have to pause at the closet, make noise and be discovered. Once outside he would set off up the tree-lined slope of the magic mountain where he lived, careful to avoid Mr Acker and his sniffing dog, who always came out to explore the night-time as he did, just after midnight.

He was four years old.

From the top of Servington Crescent in Toronto in those days when the city was filled with trees and old, solid houses, he could look down towards the mysterious lake in the sleeping silence, watch moonlight iridesce from the stained glass windows of the sandstone church he would reach to touch, and listen to the sky-high quiet and the delicate sounds of insects in summer, or in March, hear snow demobilizing its winter occupation secretly, unseen but tinkling under cover back to the harbour where everything began or ended.

One morning before he left home at one o'clock, he decided to have toast. It was one of those treacherous old flipover toasters that had to be watched carefully. But he knew how to work it. Sitting, waiting, he began to smell the rich bread begin its marvellous transformation. He licked his fingers, as his father did, so they wouldn't scorch, and then pulled the flaps out. Just right. The slices turned over. Now for the other side. But when he returned three hours later at four o'clock, his parents had come down, woken by the smell, and that was the end of the night raider. After that, they took his clothes away when he went to bed.

Fascinated by alleyways and the minutiae of garbage and bric-a-brac which inhabited them, he would explore for hours. Every sensation was irresistible to him. He would try anything. Bored by the regular food his kind mother would prepare he had to try his teeth on his brother's pasteboard maps, or on bits and pieces of exotic matter, flung out by neighbours, which he would discover in his travels; and especially (he remembers it clearly even now) he relished the delicious tang of Johnson's floorwax.

As he grew a little older he would spend long hours with friends, designing and constructing model airplanes out of balsa wood, glue sticking to his fingers like a second skin. They would fly the planes off the side of their neighbourhood hill, rubber-band motors whirring like bird-wings until they were spent and crashed into one or another of the large elms or maples — shaking down showers of autumn keys that would drift like parachutes in the wind. He was tall for his age but couldn't compete with agile friends who would stand on their heads or wiggle their ears. One thing he could do, though, was whistle through the space in his teeth. Something he still does while composing.

It was the Depression. As Harry recalls, there was never any real hardship for the family but his father was an insurance broker, not a good field to be in; and he remembers that time as characterized by a kind of tension that strung the house tight and dangled his father uncertainly for years. Very different from the situation of his grandfather, who had been city clerk for so long that he could regale the family with stories of breaking in several mayors to the chains of their office, the insecurity of a private businessman was a difficulty to be borne. His father, Russel Somers, managed to keep things together by taking on a second ''job''. He played bridge.

An excellent player, and later a good friend of the famous champion and world authority, Charles Goren, he nearly always won handily. Some nights though, the cards wouldn't run right; and there was gloom hanging like the smoke left by the departed players.

These games Harry remembers as being played in absolute silence. Later in life he could never get used to the game as a social exercise filled with small-talk, drinks and bridgemixture. Intense professionals as the contestants were, there was only the murmur of curt bids answering one another around and around the cardtable with its utilitarian plastic cover, and the deliberate slap of cards as the players unravelled the logic of each tense deal. Finally there was the passing of the money at the evening's end and he would watch to see whether his father was smiling or glum. Strong and athletic, as all the Somers seem to be, his father had been an artillery officer, a captain, during the First World War. It had greatly affected him although he never spoke of it. Harry remembers him waking screaming and sweating with nightmares.

In those days veterans' clubs, parades, and legionhall gatherings were an important part of everyday life. There were many such parades, colourful but often pitiful with old codgers, most of them well-lit, attempting to square their shoulders and keep step as in the old days but staggering from side to side instead. Just before his father died, Harry took the old man to see *Oh, What a Lovely War,* the satirical music-hall drama, which included old film clips and many of the old songs. Very quiet coming out of the theatre into a Toronto that had changed so much since he was a boy, and remembering his youth demolished by that needless war, the prime of his adulthood tied to a vicious depression, his declining years blighted with another war, his old age numbed by post-war progress, he quietly said, ''I guess we were the suckers.''

Harry's mother worried too, but managed to spread good cheer in other ways. A clever user of ''fake-books'', she played the piano almost purely by ear — always knowing the latest rag and a boogie-woogie or two. Parties would usually wind up with her at the piano, Harry and the guests singing; and she would adjust the key of the songs as they went along, so the singers wouldn't run out of pitch.

His mother also played hymns. But she was not a religious woman in the usual sense. She was a theosophist, a student of comparative religion, keenly interested in the universality of religious concepts. She had a particular interest in Eastern religions and philosophy. Harry thought it was mumbo-jumbo, but picked some of it up from her conversations and grew to understand it. Many years later her early influence would be reinforced by his second wife, Barbara Chilcott, and his travels through the East.

Another musical member of his family was an uncle who could perform the unusual feat of playing *Yankee Doodle* with his left hand, at the same time rendering *God Save The King* with his right. The effect, unfortunately, was never adopted as the Canadian National Anthem! His father always considered this man the epitome of musical genius.

Harry, himself, was much more interested in baseball and hockey. One of his childhood friends, an older boy whom Harry admired immensely, was Dudley Garret. Harry was always tall for his age so they were pretty evenly matched. They would dare each other to catch rides on the back of milk-trucks or to climb gutterpipes. Dudley was a superb hockey player, who later became a member of the New York Rangers. Once when Harry mentioned he was impressed by Shostakovich (Harry had just begun his music studies then), his grandfather, James Somers, had asked: "Shostakovich? Who's he? A new ball player?" Not exactly a breeding ground for composers.

Mr Acker, however, the one who walked his dog at midnight, was the neighbourhood eccentric that Harry admired. Harry remembers the Acker family as talented, artistic, and fascinating. On Saturday afternoons Mr Acker would listen to the opera programs on the CBC. Jim, his son, a few years older than Harry, was in the Air Force. He was lost over the North Sea during the Second World War when Harry was in his early teens.

Just before that war, in 1939, when Harry Somers was thirteen, his musical life really began. As he tells it, his ears opened suddenly. It happened at a family friend's cottage on an island in Muskoka.

Harry Somers has always loved the North and enjoyed whatever time he could spend there, looking out over the lake and listening to the long, drawn-out, haunting sound of loons. This sound he has incorporated directly in *Evocations* (written in 1966), and indirectly (as anyone listening to his music will realize) by his use of isolated 'lines' and taut silences.

It was near summer's end, his fourteenth birthday was approaching, and their host, a German doctor of the old school, brought out the cheese and the beer. He poured a glass for Harry who reached for it eagerly. He liked beer. He'd downed the dregs from glasses many a time. And here he was about to gulp his first, delicious, full glass. Just as he raised it to his mouth his mother, horrified, protested. But the good doctor saved him. ''How do you expect the boy to grow without his beer?''

Then he sat at the piano and played while Harry drank. His wife played also — Mozart, Brahms, Beethoven — ''All the old warhorses, but it was a completely new world to me at the time.'' Whether or not it was because of the beer Harry doesn't know; but he says, ''From that moment, as if I were a spark-plug waiting to be ignited, nothing would do but I had to study music, find out what it was all about, and that was it.''

THE FIRST ACT

In Harry Somers' studio hangs, in a simple frame, what appears to be a fine, abstract photograph — perhaps of Harry's pipe-smoke taken against the light. In reality it is a swirling design done by a friend of Harry's out of mushroom spores, which are carefully screened onto dark paper and fixed in beautiful random patterns that would be unobtainable in any other way. A showing of these ''mushroom-spore designs'' was held in a Toronto gallery. Sometimes a small mold eats away at the mushroom spores and gradually destroys the design. Their creator guarantees that should the wall decoration be eaten he will replace it free! This creative, sensitive, humorous artist-friend of Harry's was also his first piano instructor. A talented, perceptive teacher, Reginald Godden — examiner for the Royal Conservatory of Music, adviser to the music community, and internationally respected critic. Harry was introduced to him at a church do by Eric Aldwinckle, a war artist with the RCAF. Aware of Harry's natural ability and conscious of how late Harry was in beginning his studies, Reginald Godden managed to compress an incredible amount of music education into about two years without discouraging or boring his keen, young pupil.

In 1942, three years after Harry's ears were opened to music, Reginald Godden felt he was ready to study under John Weinzweig. Weinzweig, impressed with Godden's recommendation, remembers being particularly taken by the beautiful calligraphy of the scores Harry sent him, which he felt expressed an unusual sensitivity. Harry also showed John Weinzweig scores he had written for the piano, which Weinzweig remembers as having a strong feeling for musical colour and a tendency towards an impressionistic style. Weinzweig immediately set him to studying the techniques of classical music but was sensitive enough to realize that such a long, formal study could repress Harry's natural creative talent, since Harry kept getting ideas of his own. Accordingly he compressed this stage drastically, feeling Harry could pick it up later on. At this time John Weinzweig showed him the twelve-tone system and began directing his attention to the resources of the full orchestra, about which Harry was ignorant.

Out of this early study grew Harry Somers' first serious composition, for piano and string quartet. He was still only seventeen. Although he was determined to be a great pianist, composing as a lifetime occupation was becoming a reality to him. As he saw the composer's challenge, it meant creating the right sound symbolism by which he could make that link between his own emotional and intellectual response to life and the other person's consciousness. As with most beginning artists, his compositions tended at first towards being descriptive — a kind of music which invoked visual images or obvious emotional states. It was a stage very traditional in root but a stage which Harry felt compelled to pursue. He thought that, to become a fully developed composer, there was no use following more modern directions which came naturally and easily to him, simply because he couldn't do something else. Consequently he set to working at those things he found most difficult, biding his time, enlarging himself for the full development of his capacities, that by now he felt he would soon be ready to exploit. In this early work he often employed Baroque techniques. This interest can be heard in later compositions as well. It is interesting that the Baroque has crept into popular music recently, beginning during the sixties with the Beatles, the Swingle Singers and others.

In 1944 Harry, now aged eighteen, joined the armed forces, as did his teacher, John Weinzweig. Perhaps Harry did so because of Dudley Garret who had joined the Navy. Saying good-bye to Harry earlier, Dudley, strong and fit from playing professional hockey, had commented to his younger friend, ''I'll be all through with my career before you begin yours.'' These words came ironically, and tragically, true. Dudley's ship was blown up by a torpedo that came out of nowhere in the wide mouth of the St Lawrence. To avoid panic the U-boat raids up the St Lawrence were kept secret by the Canadian Government, and so it was a time of great confusion and uncertainty until Dudley's body was carried back to Toronto and buried there in a ceremony that still haunts Harry's mind.

In a fit of passion at that loss, Harry composed *Testament to Youth,* which he now feels was an honest but extremely naïve expression. ''Unless the symbol of the thing communicates it, it doesn't matter how powerful the impulse behind it.'' Nevertheless the piece manages to convey a tragic sense of loss and waste despite its surface simplicity.

It wasn't common knowledge then, but the War was winding down. Although Harry joined the Air Force, out of a fascination for flying that making model airplanes had given him, he was never put into formal training. It was decided he was going to become one of the entertainment personnel because of his music studies, and accordingly he was shipped from place to place in a confusing and unsettling period that lasted over a year.

After being sent to the Assiniboine region in Manitoba he was brought back to Ipperwash for basic training, which he remembers as marching through cold swamps and dodging erratic mortarfire from inept recruits. (As well as working in the laundry surrounded by mountains of stinking underwear.)

Then there was a spell in North Bay where he was trained to fire an automatic pistol and take apart Bren guns. All the time, of course, there was silly boot camp discipline, cleaning muddy boots and muddy uniforms, polishing brass buckles and silver badges, treating the webbing belts and anklets with green ''Blanco'' compound that took hours to dry, oiling the heavy, old, 303 Lee Enfield rifles with the cleaning kit stuck in the hollow butt under the brass hinge, marching endlessly at the whim of corporal or sergeant, or presenting arms to visiting brass hats who would flip their silver-tipped swagger-sticks against an offensively-dirty shoulder strap or cap-badge. There was also KP and more laundry.

At the War's close Harry was about to be sent overseas in another surprise move, to be part of the army of occupation just at the time most military personnel were being sent home. Since war was over and his composing talent was being wasted, he applied for demobilization on educational grounds.

He resumed his studies in 1946, still less than twenty-one years old. He ushered at Eaton Auditorium and got scholarships from the Conservatory to continue his studies. His interest in the piano led him to intensive study under Weldon Kilburn, who has coached, among others, the famous singer Lois Marshall. The voice as an instrument has always fascinated Harry Somers.

To expand his horizons, Harry went off to San Francisco in 1948 to study under Robert Schmitz. Harry had thirteen compositions written by then. One of these, *Strangeness of Heart,* was performed publicly at this time.

In the meantime he had met Katherine McKay, a warm, generous person. They wanted to get married. By happy coincidence Harry learned he had won an award to study composition in Paris. The award was $2,000, given by the Canadian Amateur Hockey Association. *Just enough to live on if you were frugal.* Jubilant, the young couple married and began their French honeymoon. Paris was still war-torn, most things were rationed, housing was scarce and of poor quality, but the city was alive with new hope after the long Occupation, busy rebuilding its cultural life.

Eager as they were to see everything, they had some practical problems to deal with first. Harry was determined to become a student of Arthur Honegger, to whom he had sent his manuscripts. He phoned and made an appointment. When he arrived at the impressive studio on the Boulevard de Clichy, he was greeted by Madame Honegger. No. Sorry. The maestro was unable to be in after all. Harry left. At decent intervals he returned, always to be greeted by Madame, always to be informed that her husband was not in, was not yet able to come to a decision.

Finally, filled with impatience as the weeks went by, Harry went back for the last time. He remembers thinking to himself, all right if he doesn't want to be associated with one of the greatest geniuses God has created on this Earth, then it's his misfortune! This time when Madame answered the door he stated imperiously, "I will take my manuscripts now."

Flabbergasted, she looked at him. "What?" She turned into the studio. "Well, Here's the room. I'm sure they're here somewhere."

Harry went in, picked them off the console, and as he did so, noticed a beautiful pipe-rack. In the rack was an extraordinary pipe collection, one of his interests since he'd taken up smoking the pipe a few years before. Laughing about it later, Harry said, "I always regret not studying with him because of that marvellous pipe collection of his."

Still excited by his impetuous decision to retrieve his manuscripts, still convincing himself of his genius, and knowing that Honegger's door would never open to him again now Madame had closed it behind him, he hurried on impulse down the long, wide Boulevard de Clichy until it broke up into the wild, bohemian strip-joint and brothel area of La Place Pigalle. But, dedicated young man as he was, Harry didn't pause long enough there to be distracted by the sellers of pornographic pictures or alluring young ladies leaning provocatively in doorways; instead he went straight up, unannounced, to the living quarters of another composer whose work he admired, Darius Milhaud. He ran up the ancient stairs and knocked. Milhaud came to the door himself, slightly astounded when Harry thrust his manuscripts at him and announced he wished to become his pupil.

Milhaud studied the scores. Harry waited. Muttering a little, humming to himself, Darius Milhaud finally turned to "the great, unrecognized genius". "Hum. I think, perhaps, you *might* have some talent." A bit of a let-down for his vanity, but still the master had accepted him. "Of course, you will have to join the rest of the class tomorrow and we shall see. . . . ."

Harry was downhearted. "Look," he said to his wife later, "why don't we go to San Francisco or some place where everybody goes to . . . ?"

The first few sessions were galling to Harry who, in Canada at least, was used to being treated as a bright star on a one-to-one basis by his teachers. But he stuck with it, and as the year progressed he learned to accept Milhaud's acid humour, which cut budding geniuses like himself down to size. Very perceptive and sensitive, Milhaud taught him a lot. *To expand you have to proceed in a direction other than that which is totally natural to you.* Something Harry had begun to realize earlier. It was the best thing, he feels, to happen to him at that time — to go to a person whom he didn't necessarily like. It made him look at his work much more objectively. Milhaud's favourite composer was Mozart, but he also played Brubeck records for his students to analyse.

During this vivid year of his life, accosted by all the new influences of his environment, at last in touch with the European influences he had known so little about, Harry produced four major works, most of them dedicated to Katherine. They were a string quartet, two piano sonatas, and a symphony which he completed after returning to Toronto in 1950.

SECOND ACT

Nineteen-fifty was a bad year. Back in Toronto, faced with earning a living in some way that would allow him to keep composing, Harry drove a taxicab for a while, but a minor accident while he was composing in his head ended that particular career. "It was a wonder the city and I survived it."

After seeing the respect afforded the creative artist in Europe, he was appalled by the indifference and single-minded materialism of Toronto. Maybe he and Katherine should go back to Europe where they'd at least be considered seriously. Harry spoke constantly of the French, his admiration for their culture and the courage with which they had survived the Occupation. *In Toronto you couldn't get a decent wine like a tingling Anjou or a smooth, red Bordeaux. Not only that, they hustled you out of a café the minute you'd drunk your coffee and would probably have you ejected if you dared just to sit, watch the world go by or, good grief, write music in a quiet corner* – as he'd done so many times the previous year. And people in general were inhospitable towards artists. After all, they didn't work regular hours or have any respectable ambition for material success. *Very unreliable. Not to be considered part of the human race.*

The city they'd both known was undergoing its own trauma. An unplanned, destructive development cycle was beginning in earnest. Lifeless, pastel suburbs, so ugly and untextured compared with the architecture in France, were sprawling across calm fields that had only been a walk away when he was younger. Streets were clogging with traffic, expressways pounding into ravines, and highrises crowding out those familiar human places which he had explored as a boy. His parents' house escaped but the neighbourhood's streets were widened and their trees felled. As well as all this ugliness, there was little cultural entertainment in Toronto in those days. It was the barren edge of the world. Mostly because there was a group of jazz musicians making the scene in Toronto in the fifties, Harry and his wife spent a lot of time sitting over a beer in downtown hotels.

Harry became impressed with the jazz players' ''try anything'', experimental attitude. Although the serious composer's craft is a careful one, Harry is still fascinated by the life and spontaneity of improvised music. He enjoys the extra level of awareness that develops *when all your accumulated experience and talent go into putting your musical creativity on the line in a never-to-be-repeated burst of energy.* He wrote pieces for the jazzmen – ''straight'' pieces which they would play and elaborate on, their instruments maintaining conversations with one another long into the night. By overblowing and other techniques, these musicians made Harry aware of that strange frontier of sound that lies beyond conventional instrumentation. One player, Bernie Piltch, completely exhausted himself doing a piccolo part, which Harry had written for him, on his clarinet. That was the way he wrote *Passacaglia and Fugue* (1954) – intending it for this group but having it accepted as a commission for the CBC Symphony Orchestra.

Money continued to be a problem. Commissions were few. Ordinary jobs took up too much time and drained his creative energy. But at last he found the solution, a typically difficult one, but one in which he could work his own hours. It was in the music copying business. He began, at Silverstein's, using the calligraphic talent which had so impressed Weinzweig to earn his living.

It was piece-work. The first day, his tall, thin body arched over a drafting table, he worked fourteen hours straight to pay the rent. After a while the pain in his back grew numb. When he finally straightened, his hands stiff and his shoulders cramped, he almost collapsed with the pain in his stomach from the unaccustomed position. But he somehow went back at it (earning thirty-six dollars the first week) and grew more and more skilful, churning out parts for different instruments at an incredible pace. Finally he could go in to work for one twenty-four hour stretch, usually starting late on Saturday night and ending Sunday night, to make enough to keep him for the week and allow him to compose the rest of the time or to further his musical studies. Harry always seems to see the benefit in whatever he does, no matter what it costs him. He jokes now that the skills he learned still come in handy when he has to meet commission deadlines.

Hearing Segovia one day he rushed into the best guitar teacher's studio in Toronto, guitar in hand, saying, ''I want to learn to play the guitar.''

''Oh?''

''Yes. Just like Segovia.''

In 1951 he met the composer Norm Symonds, in the copying office. He had been in the Navy, and it was he who first introduced Harry to the jazz world. Symonds, composer of a great number of works, especially opera and other co-operative ventures, remembers Harry at this time as a bit stiff, slightly difficult to get to know, with a very intellectual view of life. But Symonds found him, after that, warm-hearted, sincere, and very able to laugh at himself (making jokes at his own expense is something Harry still does), yet confident all the while that he could produce beautiful music if only he could continue to keep things together.

Other friends, too, remember Harry as having a very rough time of it. It must also have been hard on his wife, Katherine. They had no children, and Harry just managed to maintain himself and Katherine with a growing number of commissions during the fifties, working at his copying job when he needed to. His interest in guitar led to his discovering other instruments, and he began to make money on little specialty jobs, providing background music for films or television. In 1960 he even performed on stage at the Stratford Shakespearean Festival – playing a dressed-up guitar. He also played a weird electronic instrument, the theremin, to produce ghostly "descending into the vampire's lair" kinds of sounds for horror plays on radio.

This decade was a tough period for Harry Somers, now moving into his thirties, although it proved to be a tempering time in the forging of his enormous talent. Music he composed he describes as being in "standard" forms. "I was very involved with contrapuntal technique – attempting to unify conceptions of the Baroque and earlier periods, which appealed to me greatly, with high-tension elements of our own time." He was using the "tone-row" principle as the basis for his work but did not regard himself as a twelve-tone composer. The loon's lovely cry, a sound almost like a laugh, sewing together pieces of the vast, northern silence, is still in his music. "A characteristic of my work has been 'line' . . . whether you use the qualifying term 'melodic' line, or simply 'line', to signify a use of pitches in consecutive order, often completely exposed, of varying durations and intensities. This is a characteristic in some of my earliest work and is in some of my most recent. It is present in the *Suite for Harp and Chamber Orchestra* and in the *North Country Suite* for string orchestra of the 1940's. It is present in the works of the 1950's . . . with an ever-widening range of pitch and dynamic contrast, and reaches into works of the 1960's."

In 1960 he received a Canada Council senior award, which

enabled him to return to study in France. There he attended the Domaine Musical concerts of new music that Pierre Boulez was presenting. These concerts and concepts of electronic music began to "get more and more into my creative bloodstream", though his responses were intuitive rather than analytical. But the "line" he speaks about led him further afield to the monastery at Solesmes, where he absorbed the nuances of the Gregorian chant, confirming his belief that the handling of the human voice was something not yet being fully exploited.

Canada was beginning to recognize its artists as the fifties closed and the sixties began. A substantial group of Canadian composers was beginning to emerge, Harry among them. In the small, dedicated world of music they all encouraged and helped each other professionally and personally as much as they could. Harry Somers became busier with more and more work. But he had need of his friends' support.

Katherine became ill and had to undergo an operation. Some months afterwards Danuta Buczynski, the wife of composer Walter Buczynski, remembers Katherine taking up their two-month-old son onto her knee and playing gently with him as if he could have been her own. But two months later, in May 1963, Katherine died.

THE THIRD ACT

Harry Somers was alone again. But drawing on his own strong resources he kept working hard, finishing, among other things, *Stereophony for Orchestra* and *Twelve Miniatures for Voice and Instrumental Trio,* which was presented by the CBC in 1965.

His work at the CBC had put him in contact with performers and personalities such as Norma Beecroft who, besides her own compositions, was producing programs about music for the network. (One of these was a documentary on Harry himself, broadcast in 1972.) Harry, too, began radio work; his excellent speaking voice and musical knowledge made him a "natural" at the job. One of his first programs was a two-hour documentary on Stravinsky.

Ultimately everything he does influences him as a composer. Every new experience gradually is synthesized into the philosophical vision that he wants to communicate in his music. For instance, reading Harold Henderson's translations of famous Japanese haiku poems had led him to create his famous *Twelve Miniatures*. Here, the words of the sung voice part blend beautifully with the recorder, viola, and spinet. This last instrument, of great delicacy in sound, Harry had never previously used. He borrowed the small instrument from Keith MacMillan of the Canadian Music Centre to explore its range. He found the tone could not be forced or extended as it could on a piano or other keyboard instrument. Consequently, this piece uses the spinet almost as another solo voice, at times to complement the figures, at times to lead them, but always possessing its own soundspace in which to be heard. Walter Buczynski played this instrument for its premier broadcast. *Something makes a sound/ a scarecrow has fallen to the ground.* Like the writer of the haiku, Harry wanted to obtain maximum depth of feeling with minimum means.

Twelve Miniatures for Voice and Instrumental Trio has since been recorded. Reviewing this work for the *Washington Star,* Irving Lowens claims it is ''an authentic masterpiece''.

A similarly haunting composition is *Evocations,* a four-part song cycle presented by CBC radio in 1967 but composed in early 1966. Harry Somers describes how the piece grew and how it got its name: ''I jotted down words that meant something to me and lent themselves well to the voice, and the music was generated by the ideas they evoked. The first song is stimulated by a loon's cry. The words of the second build brilliant images. The third begins with a reminder of days spinning swiftly by. The fourth recalls the moods of winter.''

The loon influence he mentions is particularly interesting since it may throw light on another aspect of Harry Somers' music. Writing to Lee Hepner, then a graduate student, about ''silence'', he mentions that his use of it began as a dramatic element in the manner of Romantic composers from Beethoven on. But then he says: ''This has also gone through subtle transformations over the years till it becomes an essential element which does not break continuity, but is more like subterranean channels into which the sound disappears and from which it emerges. Another analogy might be to that of periods in which memory of sound takes over from its physical reality when the sound ceases, and memory joins to actuality when the sound returns." Anyone who has sat listening for the strange bird's call will know what he means.

By this time he had met Barbara Chilcott, the well-known actress, sister of the Davis brothers, Murray and Donald, who founded the old Crest Theatre in Toronto. Although he'd tended to laugh at his mother's ideas at the time, her theosophical studies had given him an interest in Eastern religion – an interest that Barbara shared. Even as early as 1960 Barbara had been to an Ashram with the Maharishi in India before such journeys were fashionable. She and Harry talked about new developments in the arts, especially new concepts of drama and music. Through these discussions Harry Somers came to clarify his ideas about the dramatic potential of the composer's role.

Although he had written opera before, he was elated to begin work in 1965 on *Louis Riel*. In its early stages a centennial project of the Chalmers Foundation, the idea had quickly gained additional support from other sources such as the Canada Council and the Ontario Council for the Arts. Writing about this extraordinary project, Herman Geiger-Torel, who was closely associated with it, records how Floyd Chalmers approached Mavor Moore, the writer and producer, "with the idea of commissioning an opera written specifically for the Canadian Opera Company." He remarks, "It was extremely fortunate that this approach came from a source where financial assistance was coupled with artistic knowledge."

Harry Somers was chosen to write the score for Mavor Moore's libretto, probably because of his previous success with "music drama", as he preferred to call "opera". A previous work, a ballet called *The House of Atreus,* had been favourably reviewed many times. Typical was this comment by Ron Evans, then writing for the Toronto *Telegram* and later an officer of the

Ontario Arts Council: "The best thing about *The House of Atreus* is the Somers' score. Jarringly discordant, it's full of pounding brass and ominous, ticking strings. It is terrifying and absorbing, constantly surprising and yet with a sense of rightness, of inevitability even in the midst of its eccentricity."

The Somers' score for *Louis Riel* combines a great variety of musical expression, including popular songs of the time, folk songs and electronic sounds, which issue from the four corners of the auditorium; everything underpins the drama of Mavor Moore's libretto perfectly.

Like most big productions the opera was beset by a multitude of problems as the opening-night deadline neared. September 23, 1967. For Harry the time was complicated by the fact that he and Barbara were arranging their marriage that same month. But it all fell together perfectly and the first-night performance received a standing ovation.

Canadian papers gave it rave reviews. But the raves also came from other quarters. For instance, the *San Francisco Examiner* said, "Canadian composer Harry Somers shows great and daring ability in a *Riel* score that makes a blend of many flavours of contemporary and avant-garde idioms." And an article in *Opera Welt*, headed "Even in Canada they compose opera", stated: "Somers made the material all his own by completely surrendering to its force and thus gaining complete possession of it. The result is an advanced piece of music, exciting in its uncompromising attitude."

Coming in for particular notice was the lullaby sung by Riel's wife at the beginning of the third act – a piece in its own right called "Kuyas" (long ago). Zelda Heller of the Montreal *Gazette* commented that it "completely transfixed the public. Here is an aria that can hardly help finding its way into the permanent concert repertoire, a work that gains in conviction and strength with every performance and every hearing."

Riel was performed more times in one year than most operas are in a lifetime, and its success was such that it will undoubtedly continue to be performed in the future. Centennial Year performances included a presentation at Expo in Montreal. A television production of *Riel* came in October 1969. Herman Geiger-Torel remained with the opera, handling the myriad production problems that inevitably cropped up.

Most composers and musicians become teachers at one time or another. Harry Somers came to teaching late since he supported himself almost entirely by his work. As with all his experiences he approached it with a sense of curiosity and originality. In 1968-69, C. Laughton Bird, Co-ordinator of Music for the North York Board of Education, invited him to participate as a consultant in a project co-funded by the Ontario Arts Council and his Board. Given free rein to meet classes, discuss programs with teachers, perform, or observe, he came to many of the same conclusions about music education as his colleague Murray Schafer.

Schools, Somers found, suffer from terrific pressures of numbers and of finances. Because it takes so many years to develop skills sufficiently to give students satisfaction in traditional ways, the number of children who manage to attain any degree of proficiency in music is small compared with those who drop out. What education should try to do is to deal with ways to manipulate sound, so students can get a kick out of sound, have their curiosity stimulated, so that their soundsense will develop and be free to move in any experimental direction. Music education is too forced, too specialized, too soon. And adults tend to hang onto the pleasant, sentimental traditions in music with which they feel comfortable and familiar.

Harry Somers rejects the idea of music as a ''frill''. In fact he can see sound studies as having a central place in the curriculum as schools move into interdisciplinary instruction. *Look at how integral it could be to a study of mathematics, physics, electronics, even language studies (by training the ear); and in all fields concerning movement (athletics, the dance, and so on). Then, of course, there is history. Isn't it just as important to know what people listened to at a certain period as it is to know what they dressed in or fought with?*

The notion of music as an esoteric artform was another problem. Popular music should never be ignored. *The whole field becomes so infected with petty busyness that way. Look at the Baroque period. Bach didn't think of himself as somehow apart from society. He was forced to turn it out and people listened and loved it and demanded more.*

In co-operation with other musicians, especially Murray Schafer, and the Ontario Arts Council's special projects department headed by Linda Zwicker, Harry Somers helped establish "The Music Box", a creatively-stimulating learning package that schools can buy for their students.

He learned more subtle things as well, to do with the response that comes from an audience; something the actor knows about. Now he began to feel the dramatic tension and excitement that Barbara had discussed with him so often. *Yes. In any performance the audience becomes a component of the whole event.*

Improvisation begins to explore this aspect. An extraordinary work involving, at one point, tossing tennis balls into a grand piano, it opens up the possibilities of spontaneous improvisation in a carefully controlled schema in which the players become actors as well, responding to the events that occur on stage and in the audience. In this score the composer is widening his function to include that of a stage director.

Lecturing also brought Harry Somers to create a work concerned almost entirely with phonics, *Voiceplay.* Using the dramatic possibilities of the lecture form, the "singer", after giving a "sound lecture" composed of sung vowels, answers "sound questions" made by the audience. The "listeners" are induced to respond spontaneously by "sound suggestions" that the composer has created, in a series of "acts" which parallel those common emotional states a lecturer projects at various stages of his discourse.

FINALE

Harry Somers' studio is in a small bachelor apartment on Hillsboro Avenue in midtown Toronto. The natural light pours in through a large, square window onto a large, square, teak desk, its top finely finished with inset brass hinges. The top covers a storage space that will hold large sheets of paper. The small room is made cosy and quiet with shag broadloom in a blend of gold and red, fall colours. A comfortable, tweed easy-chair welcomes visitors. Harry pours beer in the small kitchenette off to the right. Also to the right is an apartment-size piano. By the opposite wall is a new acquisition that Harry experiments with. It's a German-made drafting-board with a special feature that makes drawing parallel lines a matter of pressing a button like a tabulator on a typewriter. It's easier to use this device for his scores, he claims, rather than the usual pre-lined paper, because he only uses the traditional staff intermittently, covering most of the paper with other symbols and instructions. In a matching teak bookshelf sit completed scores in their neat, yellow envelopes, his italics signature in india ink written on the outside.

Harry talks about how he had been left working on scores for the TV series, ''Images of Canada'', while Barbara went to Italy. She was there on business of her own but was helping to organize a concert of Canadian music which had grown out of Harry's previous stay there with her during 1970 and 1971. He had been in Italy on an $18,000 Italian cultural fellowship awarded through the Canadian Cultural Institute in Rome, acting on advice from the Canada Council. Earlier negotiations for the concert took a lot of work, in which Harry was assisted by Japanese soprano Michiko Hirayama, who had been living in Rome for seventeen years. The singer had visited Toronto a few years before and had become excited about music developments in this country. The 1972 concert opened more ears in Europe to Canadian music than ever before.

The smoke curls from his pipe against the bright summer light. Harry swivels in his desk-chair and watches the amber beer glowing in the glass he is lifting. He wears a comfortable, roll-neck cardigan, which frames his sculptured face. He's thinner than usual. It is not long since he has recuperated from an attack of malaria that he caught while he and Barbara were coming home from Italy by way of the East. The illness, for him, was more an interesting experience than a fight for life. He laughs, remembering the incongruity of 105 degree fevers alternating with freezing chills and his teeth clattering like castanets.

Throughout the East there was uninterrupted sunshine, tea in a glass, carved stone cities, robed figures in far, brown fields, also the Eastern traditions of hospitality and accessibility, great men approachable by anyone. Especially was this true in Chandigarh. The head of its huge school of architecture dropped everything to spend the day showing them his amazing mid-twentieth-century city, designed by the French architect Le Corbusier, and he insisted they stay at his house so he could show them what it felt like to experience the city at night. Then there were all the new sounds they encountered all over the East: in Bali, music unlike any other, and in Kashmir, the songs of a wedding.

As it is with his wife, time for meditation is important to him; but like most geniuses he seems capable of orchestrating meditation with creative involvement in his work, seemingly able to be reflective and involved at the same time – always finding a minute here, a minute there, in his busy life, to smoke his pipe, lean back and relax.

When he begins work composing again, he will walk around the studio as he often does at home, humming, singing notes out loud, occasionally using the piano keyboard, sitting down, finally, to make notes on the drafting board. He walks, now, over to Reginald Godden's spore pattern, studies it, searches for traces of mites eating the spores, finds none, turns into the kitchen compartment, opens the knife drawer for a bottle opener, picks up a wad of tissue paper, carefully unfolds it and takes out a beautiful medal. Companion of the Order of Canada. This country's highest award.

Not so long ago, in Government House, he had stood with forty other eminent people from every profession, waiting to be honoured by the Governor-General. With flawless dignity, Roland Michener invested each one of them, adding his own personal tribute for which he had no need to refer to notes since he knew each one's accomplishments so well.

Harry puts the red-and-white ribbon around his neck. The heavy gold-and-white enamelled cross dangles over his woollen cardigan. He takes it off, after a while, covering it carefully with the tissue, placing it back in the drawer. He has it wrapped that way because, at a celebration afterwards with friends, he lost the box he was supposed to keep it in.

He looks down from his own high tower over the polluted, noisy city, blighted with muzak; and he remembers the Muezzin's clear call, every morning and every evening – commanding the silences – as the loon's cry does over Canada's still and perfect lakes.

john beckwith

ambour-ines, the stone chimes, the ba-tons and tiger-clappers.

The tambour-ines, the stone chimes, the ba-tons and tiger-clapp

BELL

ines, the stone chimes, the ba-tons and tiger-clappers. rapid cresc.

AVES rapid cresc...

The tambour-ines, the stone chimes, the ba-to

IND-HARP mp

SHARON FRAGMENTS

This is his generating image:
a Child of Peace
illumined in the hollow gem
called Sharon Temple,
where his students' faces too
peer upward lit
by heartfelt antique music (they imagine
it is ringing down
sweet women's voices
making light its burdens).

This lighthouse peacespace where
a host of candles rayed
against Ontario's ignorant early nights
and beckoned travellers, the great
Mackenzie once who claimed,
''Their choirs and music are
unequalled anywhere in Upper Canada.''
A visitor from England, 1830, wrote,
''It struck me as remarkable
these country farmers could
have got it up so well.''

He leads his students past a Jacob's ladder
(dangerous to climb it now ghosts only
roam its gallery) to where the barrel-
organ rests, moved from the simple
meeting-house, restored and since
retuned by Keith MacMillan.
(These Sharon fragments made
whole melodies again.)
Its cylinders trip levers for its pipes
(one cranks by hand).
A common thing in England but

the first in Canada and built
by Coates, an organ-maker, military
man and talented musician
sick of death who met
with David Willson founder
of this sect. Ex-Quaker Willson
loved all beauty music painting light.

Professor Beckwith fits a cylinder.
They crank. There's something wrong.
"I think we've wound it backwards."
So they laugh. They try again.
A simple song.

PETER SUCH

"Life inspires all our actions. The body can feel
nothing, but it touches the mind; therefore it is
the man within that is the life of the body, and
exists in all our limbs."

*David Willson's words used by John Beckwith
in his work* Sharon Fragments

Ot the Western end of this long, thin line of culture called Canada, in the city of Victoria on its calm Pacific island, John Beckwith was born in 1927. Radio was new. Like the giant caribou of Eskimo mythology it vaulted across the Northern Borealis, carrying to him opera *(Tristan and Isolde* with Flagstad), and Toscanini's Beethoven cycle, as well as the New York Philharmonic and Kay Kyser. He could listen. He once wrote: "I was a *fan*. When I came to Toronto at age eighteen, I found I knew more operas and symphonies than most of my fellow music students, although in Victoria there had seldom been any live performances by orchestras or opera companies." In the public library he would ferret out scores of upcoming programs if they could be found. He was in his early teens, then.

Ever since he was six years old he'd been involved with music. Piano lessons. But he wasn't a prodigy. No one pushed him. He enjoyed it. He also sang in the unusually accomplished, Anglican Cathedral choir in Victoria. Stanley Bulley, remembered by Beckwith as cantankerous, cranky, romantic, directed it. He was a catalyst in young John's emotional involvement with music. The choir performed the Mozart Requiem, the *Messiah,* and other complicated work, but the music sung was never more contemporary than Vaughan Williams.

He and his sister, Sheila, studied piano with Gwendoline Harper, who later went to teach at Eastern Washington State University. She lived across the street and devoted herself to her pupil John more than one hour a week. She, too, stimulated his curiosity and his growing musical awareness; although, in terms of pure technique, he was later almost completely indebted to Alberto Guerrero, the Chilean master at the Royal Conservatory of Music in Toronto.

John Beckwith was also a scholar. But his interests were so wide-ranging that he was never quite the top pupil in regular subjects. Besides his music, he acted, and edited the school paper. When he graduated he wasn't eligible for one of the usual awards, but his teachers invented a new category for him:

"for achievement in drama, journalism and music."

His initiative was probably his parents' fault. Both took their commitment to parenthood seriously. They really enjoyed having children and bringing them up. They created a cultural environment which, though in some ways protective, did not spoil their children. Both were active people and set a good example. Involvement with life came naturally.

His father was "a small-town, general lawyer". During the Second World War he worked for the Canadian Government as an expropriation expert, using his knowledge of the area to advise on acquisitions for government contracts.

John worked summers in his office as a "Joe boy", running errands, getting coffee for the staff, as well as filing and more important duties. Later his father came much into demand as an arbiter in labour disputes because of his reputation for fairness and coolness. He was very respected by both sides because he listened well and genuinely sympathized. John feels his father's only fault, and one which harmed only himself, was that he was "over-controlled".

His father died in 1958, and in 1962 John dedicated an orchestral work to his memory. In his program notes to this piece which he called *Flower Variations and Wheels*, he says: "I regard it not as a formal elegy or dirge at all, but rather as a piece of music he might have liked. . . . *Flower Variations* uses a theme which is a kind of memento of a past era – a nostalgic and homely melody announced first of all in a solo flute. This piece could be taken to embody my sentimental memories of Victoria. In the same fashion, *Wheels* perhaps recalls the vigour of cycling days there – cycling having been just about my only athletic accomplishment as a teenager."

His mother, dark, tall, good-looking, was bright and slightly bossy. Before her marriage she had been a teacher. This experience led her to become involved in the early Parent-Teacher movement in Victoria. She felt that school affairs were not being well handled and that the School Board was showing signs of corruption. There had been no elections for years. Not interested in politics, she nevertheless ran for election to the

School Board because she regarded improved administration as essential.

It was a lively campaign which John, then about eleven years old, became caught up in. He distributed pamphlets, helped choose election pictures for his mother's posters and ran around quelling panic when the pace became hectic.

The night she won there was a celebration, of course. His mother and father brought the party to a hysterical conclusion with their joint performance of a favourite piano duet known as *The Bright as a Button Polka,* which had everybody tripping over one another and collapsing on the furniture.

They were both musical people. His father had a good baritone voice, and knew most of Gilbert and Sullivan by memory. For a time he conducted a church choir. His mother, too, besides playing the piano, sang alto in church choirs and ''encouraged us as youngsters to listen to Walter Damrosch's radio talks (Good afterNOON, my young friends!). The family had also inherited an old Edison phonograph and a supply of ''inch-thick'' records. ''Meyerbeer's *Coronation March* was one item I recall.

''From about age eight, I think, I had the idea I wanted to be a composer – mainly, at that time, in order to become very, very famous!''

While the lone artist Emily Carr explored the Charlotte Islands and the coastal sounds, her friend Ruth Humphrey was teaching literature at Victoria College, at that time an affiliate college of the University of British Columbia. John had a choice of three things: begin an arts course at UBC in Vancouver, go to Washington University for a music course, or take the arts course at Victoria College in Victoria. The third was the one he chose.

Finding him in her class, Ruth Humphrey, who years later would become professor emeritus, directed and channelled his interests in such a way that he quickly learned the rigorous honesty of true intellectualism. ''She got me going on reading and writing. She was critical in the best sense – she would slam me for basic things – had I really questioned, had I really thought, had I read so and so? It was good for me because up till then I'd been intellectually spoiled.''

John Beckwith has been much influenced by Emily Carr. Perhaps because of his slight connections with her in place and time. Emily's sister, Alice, was an acquaintance of his mother's, and he remembers, as a child of seven, that he spent the summer as a boarder in her private school, which Emily visited. He remembers an early show of Emily Carr's paintings which was held in a tent-like structure. She didn't seem terribly interested in selling them and, of course, her fame came very late in her life.

Emily was a writer, too, of rare ability. John's interest in literature, particularly Canadian literature, has been a distinguishing mark of his work and he read Emily's writings while still at University. His own writing ability found professional expression later in the unusually perceptive music criticism which he wrote for the *Globe and Mail* and the *Toronto Star*. He was also the writer of an amazing number of articles on various subjects for books and journals, and helped edit important publications about music and musicians.

Harry Hickman was another teacher who influenced him strongly. He taught French and used to talk at length about French songs, often playing records of them in class. It was a unique college situation, in which pupil and teacher could become close and learning could be exciting. Perhaps the building itself had something to do with it. It was a large masonry structure called Craigdarroch Castle, built by one of the early Victorian coal-barons. Taken over by the city for taxes, it had been various things in its time. It is now the home of the Victoria Conservatory of Music. The wooden floors were inlaid and a fireplace was in every room.

He did well that year and edited the College annual — drawing on his experience as editor of his high-school newspaper. He was still only seventeen.

That same year, 1945, he won a Royal Conservatory of Music scholarship to study piano. He decided to do so under Alberto Guerrero at the Conservatory in Toronto. Fortunately, the same year as he won the scholarship, the University of Toronto accepted him into the second year of a degree course in the Faculty of Music. He decided to leave home for Toronto.

That summer, before heading for Toronto, he attended the Banff School of Fine Arts, to take the theatre course. When he arrived in Toronto he immediately followed this up by becoming associated with the Hart House Theatre Group. It was post-war reconstruction time. Civilization, as Hugh MacLennan expresses it in *The Watch That Ends The Night,* had been shown to be a fragile thing – something never to take for granted. The students, consequently, many of them veterans, were a committed group of mature people. John Beckwith was just eighteen. He took part in the first Hart House production staged after the War.

Other people he came to know were poet and dramatist James Reaney, with whom he would collaborate for many of his most important works; poet Phyllis Gottlieb; and Robert Weaver, Director of Radio Arts at the CBC, a critic, and *Tamarack Review* editor. There was also Norman Depoe, the television news personality; Glenn Gould, the famous pianist, who also studied with Guerrero; Harry Somers and Harry Freedman, both well-known, influential composers; and Mary Morrison. Mary used to sing John's songs while training to become the accomplished performer she now is. With such a group in one place at one time it is no wonder that John felt himself part of a cultural renaissance.

Slight, small, quick, with tremendous energy, John Beckwith managed to pursue all those things that interested him. Besides drama, these included his studies with Guerrero. These lessons produced some of his most profound musical experiences. Every so often, during lesson discussions, Alberto Guerrero would give his own "readings" of "Bach, Mozart, Chopin, Debussy, and other wonderful music. . . . These performances were always casual and unforced; they came up as a mere adjunct of my studies, it seemed – but their effect was deeply memorable."

In other hours there were his regular classes and some journalism for *The Varsity.* (Mark Harrison, who much later became editor of the *Toronto Star,* edited the student newspaper at that time.) Besides these things John continued writing his own musical compositions.

In 1947, aged twenty, he received his Bachelor of Music degree with the highest marks of his year. By this time he was certain he wanted to lead a creative, artistic life, preferably as a composer. But why a composer? In those early days he felt he knew why; but he would tell his friends, ''I can't put it into words.'' Later he tended to say it had to do with discovery: ''I'm just plain curious what the result of musical impulses will be when they're carried through the complicated mill of training, technique, personal instinct and choice.'' Then, as now, however, there was that problem of being allowed by society to make a decent living out of artistic enterprise. Composing, Beckwith feels, ''seems to be my function – and it's not my fault it's a function that has about as much apparent relevance to modern life as the manufacture of buggy wheels.''

His friend, James Reaney, was by now also committed to an artistic life as a poet, dramatist and literary editor. He and John held lengthy discussions about the problem that kind of life presented in those times. The rest of the world seemed to be purely interested in successful careers and marriages. ''Can a man successfully combine marriage and an artistic career?'' was the question they once jokingly discussed – it could have been the title of a woman's magazine article. But the question was really only a tentative one because the temper of those times was such that they felt a certain inevitability about what they did; energy was expended more in doing something well rather than in wondering whether it should be done at all. Once, John spent two weeks studying *King Lear* intensively because he knew a production was coming to town and he wanted to make sure he knew everything he could before seeing the performance. A performance which, because Stratford and television didn't exist at that time, he might not see again for many years.

John Beckwith has a great deal of sympathy for today's young people, and an understanding of the complex problems they face – even though they were not the concerns of his own youth. And although as Dean he is concerned with the ultimate administrative responsibility of the Faculty of Music of the University of Toronto, he makes time to teach a regular course and to tutor individual students at the graduate level. Students say he is always extremely well prepared, an excellent resource person who "doesn't talk off the top of his head." He's "very fair, very just, very interesting, very understanding. Always."

During his last year at the University, a talented young actress he had known in Victoria came to Toronto to study at the Canadian Theatre School, run by Ernest Sterndale Bennett. He and she fell in love, and not stopping to analyse the relationship to death, decided to get married. Although she became mother of their four children — Robin-Jane, Jonathan, Simon and Lawrence — Pamela Terry (she uses her maiden name) still maintains an active career as a director and producer in Toronto theatre.

Before their marriage in 1950, John Beckwith set out to make a living as a composer and musician as best he could. Fortunately he won several music festival awards and the Heintzman piano scholarship, and he wrote reviews intermittently for the *Globe and Mail* during 1948 and 1949. It all helped. He also gave recitals in Ontario, and in Vancouver and Victoria — running back and forth across the country on that thin, cultural line.

At "home" in Toronto, however, John Beckwith couldn't afford to have a piano to practise on. He was still, in 1948 and 1949, taking instruction from Alberto Guerrero, as well as lessons in conducting. The Conservatory hired him occasionally as a "rehearsal piano" and he played in local studios as an accompanist for singers in recital. The Opera School at the Conservatory was opening at that time, and he also spent hours coaching students in opera.

There was still no real practice piano for him until the Conservatory, expanding enormously in the post-war years, decided it needed a house-bulletin, an information and news magazine which would be under the supervision of a publicity person. John was ideal for the job since he had a tremendous knowledge of music, was familiar with the institution, and had a recognized writing ability. His title was "Director of Publicity". The pay, however, was dreadfully inadequate since budget considerations had not taken the position into account. John made a deal. Give him a small office and put a piano in it! At the time he was desperate to practise for what turned out to be an outstanding lecture-recital on Bach's "Goldberg Variations", which won rave acclaim in Toronto early in 1950.

His friendship with Reaney began to take on creative substantiality as soon as he graduated. In 1949 they collaborated on a very successful piece that Beckwith still recalls fondly: it was *The Great Lakes Suite*. Previously, John had broken into "professional" composition with a series of five songs, based on Chinese poems, entitled *Five Lyrics of The T'ang Dynasty*. Published in 1949, they were the first of his works to receive a public performance and had won him a CAPAC award. He followed those with a suite of seven pieces for piano duet, *Music for Dancing*, which he later orchestrated.

The Great Lakes Suite was presented by the CBC for the Sunday Concert Series. Each of six poems by Reaney catches the poet's impression of each lake. Superior is Lord of the others, who are "inferior". He is haughty, cold, and grey with "iron shores". Michigan is distinguished by the windy jangle of Chicago. Huron is a coy Indian maiden. Tiny Lake St Clair is made notable by the trials of a swimming bear, trying to breathe the polluted air; Erie is "weary/of washing the dreary/crowds of the cities that line my shores"; and finally, in a moody, reflective break from the clownish satire of the others, Ontario shows its vastness, its irresistible waves, to the onlooking poet – who realizes he can only be "a megaphone to their blue green blue noise".

Since the lakes were personified, John Beckwith chose to write the suite for both male and female voices. Piano, clarinet and cello added keyboard, woodwind and string colour-ranges with minimal means. Critics spoke of the qualities of "wit and cryptic clarity" which distinguished the music, and which, in many following pieces, established John Beckwith's individual "signature". The piece could have easily been spoiled by the wrong pacing, if the score had not been consistently sharp and his transitions from one song to the next kept ruthlessly uncluttered. Surprise endings contribute to the fast-moving, satirical, witty punch of the piece and lead to the contrasting, reflective mood of the last song which, like the great rush of the vast waterway itself, pushes quietly, inevitably on past the listener into a silent horizon.

The piece also contains a few ''musical quotations'' – phrases and sounds from other musical periods or styles that cause the listener to respond in a predictable way.

In succeeding collaborations with Reaney, John Beckwith began to work out a ''collage'' technique more and more, extending it to include environmental sounds, ordinary speech, and dramatic images. Reaney himself was a great influence in this respect: as a dramatist, he too was becoming more and more interested in happenings and mosaic structures. This first collaboration was the only one in which John Beckwith worked from a formal typescript that Reaney had ready. Unlike most composers who draw on a standard body of literature for inspiration and ''set'' or reconstruct it for their own musical purposes, Beckwith believes in real collaboration.

With James Reaney he has been particularly fortunate since Reaney ''understands music from the inside.'' Usually they sit down together and discuss the aims of the piece, or what they are trying to achieve, before setting a word or a note down on paper. Fortunately, too, Reaney has the kind of professional personality that doesn't see criticism as a threat. Beckwith feels that Reaney is almost careless in protecting his ''inventions'', always ready to throw away whatever Beckwith doesn't like, coming back the next day with a new version that usually both find more satisfactory. For instance, Beckwith will explain that he can only ring so many changes on a particular rhythm. Reaney will then vary his rhythms so that there will be more to work with.

Among other works done about the time of *The Great Lakes Suite* were *Four Songs to Poems by e.e. cummings*, commissioned by Lois Marshall for her Toronto début; *Four Songs to Poems by Edith Sitwell;* and two songs to poems by Colleen

Thibaudeau (a Canadian writer and friend). "Serenade", one of the latter songs, won a prize in the CBC song-writing contest for 1950.

That same year, his friend Harry Somers wrote to him from Paris. Harry was there on a $2,000 Canadian Amateur Hockey Association arts scholarship. What Harry told him about the European music scene convinced John he should try to get there. In those days there was no Canada Council or Ontario Arts Council, and only a few bodies were able to give anything but meagre awards. For some reason connected with the Amateur Hockey Association's non-profit status, the Association at that time had been eager to direct some of its funds towards artistic and charitable ends. Harry's scholarship had been the first of its kind. Would the Association repeat its award? There was no harm in trying. Yes. The award was granted.

He and Pamela immediately set their wedding date to coincide with the trip. They would have their honeymoon in Paris.

John had made up his mind to study with Nadia Boulanger. This famous teacher of both performing artists and composers had broken with the regular Paris Conservatoire to form what she called her "American School". Internationalist in outlook, fluent in many languages besides French and English, she taught many well-known American composers before the Second World War. Her pupils included Aaron Copland, who has an essay on her methodology and music in his book, *Copland on Music*.

The life of this woman of amazing passion and vitality has spanned several generations of famous musicians, since she was born in the 1880's. Even when over ninety she was a guest conductor and lecturer at Yehudi Menuhin's Bath Music Festival in England, a country with many previous associations for her. Her early life was marred by the tragic death of her brilliant sister, Lilli, at age twenty-three. As every year, she held a memorial service for her in Trinité church while John and Pamela were there. Like her other students, John received a black-edged invitation to attend.

John Beckwith himself retains a sense of ritual and magic and could respect such a practice continuing for so many years, but perhaps partly because he found Trinité to be the most senti-mentalized, overdecorated nineteenth-century church in Paris, he was not won over to what he felt was Nadia Boulanger's style of expressive emotionalism.

His first year as her private pupil was exciting and enjoyable, however. Because she had been exposed to so many different styles of music and musicians, Mlle Boulanger had a tolerant, eclectic outlook, and dealt not so much with the style of the music as with the style of the person; she wanted to stretch her pupils to the limits of their capacities.

On Wednesdays he would go to the weekly gathering of her students called the ''Mercredi Musical'', which she held in her apartment. It was a huge place, panelled, hung elaborately with drapery and festooned with mementoes. There they would sing, play, and analyse music ensembles. There were two pianos, and often, ecstatic at the beauty of the music, she would push one or other of the student performers off his stool and fly into the piece herself. Her whole life seemed to pour out into the music.

As with many geniuses, her dedication to absolute perfection gave her a somewhat authoritarian demeanour which John found, as the year progressed, always made him a little resistant to her criticism of his work. He did, however, begin a second year under her tutelage before his own developing maturity and self-confidence caused him to feel that he had learned all he could from Nadia Boulanger, and that there were certain philosophical prejudices in her musical outlook that were not compatible with his own. In addition there was that question of their differing temperaments; she very emotionally expressive, he more given to wittiness and reserve. One day one of her favourite pupils, Dinu Lipatti, died. The Mercredi Musical that week became what to John was a lugubrious ceremony of eulogy, at which they sang and played part of Lipatti's last recording while Mlle Bou-langer was constantly in tears. Although he respected her depth of emotion enormously, John Beckwith found he simply could not join in, could not respond the same way.

Pamela, who already knew much French, had quickly become expert at the language through her studies at the Alliance française. She was soon involved with a theatrical crowd that staged Gertrude Stein's *Yes Is For A Very Young Man,* a play about the French resistance movement. The success of this venture caused the young couple to decide to remain in France. Their first summer Pamela had a job acting and stage managing in a touring company that was to tour US occupation posts in Austria and Germany. John went along too, since he had landed a small part in the production.

After ceasing his studies with Nadia Boulanger, John spent his time composing, practising, becoming involved in drama with Pamela, and later travelling.

THE LINE UP AND DOWN

By the fall of 1952 they were ready to return to Canada. "It was a classic situation. We landed in Toronto broke and pregnant!" But John Beckwith is a person who can say about himself that he can't recall any time since he was twelve that he didn't have "at least three full-time jobs", and the capacity to do many things diligently and creatively has always brought him all sorts of projects, many of which others didn't particularly want to do. And always the particular job was used by him to further his craft in one way or another.

Picking up again on his writing skills he started once more to write music criticism, often combining the necessity of regular concert-going with a freelance job as concert manager. Incidentally he gave a few lectures on Wagner, continued his opera coaching, and did the odd recital, although it was difficult to find time for practising. Somehow he also managed to function as the secretary of the Canadian League of Composers, which John Weinzweig had founded (Harry Somers had been its first secretary). Lastly, Arnold Walter at the Faculty of Music asked him to fill in on a one-hour-a-week course. A measure of the Faculty's confidence in him was that the course was a senior one (third-year) in analysis.

At this time, while the Beckwiths were living under the sweet smell of the Neilson Chocolates factory, Pamela managed to help make ends meet by doing a few odd jobs in theatre. Robin-Jane was born in April 1953. Jonathan followed in November 1954.

All this time ideas were growing like secret flowers in John's mind for an opera which he and James Reaney were determined to produce. However, this opera, called *Night Blooming Cereus,* didn't take final form for years. It was eventually finished in 1958 (it had been started in 1953). Their confidence in its worth inspired them to take the risk of putting it on stage rather than being satisfied with a CBC radio broadcast only. By cutting corners financially they managed to see their way clear to producing it. Beckwith took the brunt of the arrangements, rehearsals and other problems because Reaney was in Winnipeg. It was exhausting and frustrating work but also an act of faith in a country where such ventures are normally doomed before they see the spotlights. The opera was actually produced in 1960, financed mostly by money John Beckwith had made from his music criticism for the *Toronto Star.* (He worked for the *Star* in two sessions: 1959-62 and 1963-65.) Although he had kept at "his own work" whenever he could, the period of about four years of intense activity at the close of the fifties kept him from doing more than a small amount of serious composing.

The artistic problem had intensified (although the economic one diminished) after Robin-Jane was born. In 1953 a CBC producer asked him if he would be interested in applying for a job that had come open in radio continuity. He applied and was accepted. Because of his commitment at the Faculty of Music and his other projects, John, although on salary, was allowed to choose his own hours.

He found he now had the freedom of both the Faculty of Music Library and the CBC Library. And moving into the centre of the city gave him much more time to spend in research and listening. Eventually he found himself doing two radio series a week: "Music in our Time" (1953-56) and "Music of The Church" (summertime: 1954-57). Later he began "The World of Music" (1956-64).

This workload became even heavier. At Christmas 1954

another vacancy arose at the Faculty, and John agreed to take on what was at least half a regular teaching load. At the same time he made an arrangement with the CBC to continue his work there. The teaching was tremendously hard work, particularly as he'd had little training in some of the subjects, and to teach something one has to learn it completely before entering the classroom. He learned a great deal through it all.

Though still working for the CBC, the following summer he became a full-time teacher at the Faculty. At this time he began to take graduate work in the newly-formed graduate department of the Faculty and studied under Myron Schaeffer, Harvey Olnick, and John Weinzweig. He particularly enjoyed the orchestration part of the course that Weinzweig gave. John completed his Master of Music in Composition in 1961.

In August 1956, a year after his full-time appointment, Pamela gave birth to their third child, Simon. He then quit his formal job with the CBC: he would now do a program series on a freelance rather than a salaried basis. Often at night he would sit in either library – listening to music and formulating his programs – and he developed an enormous stock of musical knowledge. This listening habit is something which he feels he has let slip in more recent years.

In the light of John Beckwith's "style" (if such a wide range of expression can be categorized that way) this period of time obviously contributed to many of the "Ivesian" features in his compositions. Charles Edward Ives, the famous American composer, as a boy had often heard several military bands playing at once; in later years as a composer he developed a collage technique whose atonalities derived from the simultaneous juxtaposition of essentially tonal elements. In this way he anticipated the "McLuhanesque" notion of the mosaic-contrapuntal structures of modern art – those attempts to involve all the senses and capacities at once in an interplay the EST (Latin: it is) people would call "simulsensory". In music terms, these techniques conflict philosophically with the pigeonholing "harmoniousness" of nineteenth-century music which, by restricting tonality, directs the listener's attention more to having his "eyes on the finish'' (as Bertold Brecht would put it) rather than ''on the course''.

But John Beckwith's contrapuntal technique is mostly linked, in his compositions, with his use of the human voice. Discussing, in 1961, his interest in composing ''musical collages to go with poetry and drama'', he described his aim. ''A small group of instrumentalists are given timed but otherwise totally unrelated passages which, on cue, they will start or stop playing: the aim is to provide stimulating but non-competitive sound-textures to go with the rhythms of verse; the problem has always interested me greatly.''

A look at almost any one of Beckwith's vocal scores will show how cleverly he has apportioned the textual material to different voice-parts in such a way that phrases repeat, collide, echo or contrast with each other. The Estonian-Canadian composer and critic, Udo Kasemets, has written: ''Beckwith has an uncanny ability for not only setting words to music, but also for portraying musically what emerges from between and beyond the lines. He knows how to capture in sounds the whole gist of the texts as well as how to underline each detail.''

Only a person with a great literary sensitivity could have been so successful in this way. Besides his collaborations with James Reaney, there were others, with other outstanding Canadian poets. Among these projects were *The Trumpets of Summer* (1964) with text by Margaret Atwood and *Place of Meeting* (1966-67) with text by Dennis Lee. *The Trumpets of Summer* collaboration actually began with Jay Macpherson, poet and Professor of English at Victoria College (University of Toronto), who had just collaborated with him on the cantata *Jonah* (1963). In several discussions they roughed out the structure of the composition in terms of the commission, which was to celebrate the 400th anniversary of Shakespeare's birth. They decided it should illuminate the ways in which Shakespeare has become part of the Canadian experience. Professor Macpherson suggested that Margaret Atwood, then a colleague of hers, could do the actual writing; and after more talks amongst the three of them Margaret Atwood produced the first version of the text two weeks later. With slight alterations each suggested, the piece grew from there. Her text was witty and satirical, with references to all those aspects of Canadian life wherein Shakespeare figures: in school, in amateur productions, in showy, gala evenings, in reflections on the course of man's life and his death. Her words were subtle transformations and parodies of well-known quotations from the Bard and were divided contrapuntally among the chorus, speakers, and two soloists.

About his music for the piece, John Beckwith writes: "The mixtures of speaking, singing and instrumental sounds are sometimes quite free, in the manner of the radio-collages I have been composing in recent years to go with texts by James Reaney. The music employs two different twelve-note series, one scalic, the other of mixed intervals (one 'Elizabethan', the other contemporary). . . . Movement Two, innocent of such sophistries, serializes its own modal, opening phrase. There is some free tonal material, including a homely musical quotation, in the 'frame' sections of Movement Four."

Critics, hearing the finished piece, were enthusiastic. Kenneth Winters wrote in the Toronto *Telegram* (March 7, 1966): "On the purely technical level, it handles the mixture of speech, chorus, and semi-chorus, solo singing and instrumental sound, without evading the issue by just giving them to us one at a time and yet without making a mish-mash either. There is no congestion. All is deft, all is intelligible; the text is always enhanced." And about a later performance of this work *Toronto Star's* critic William Littler commented (February 17, 1969): "Rather than turn out a stuffy *pièce d'occasion*, the composer stuck his tongue firmly into his cheek and dipped his pen in cider. The result is thirty-six minutes of musical and literary irreverence. *The Trumpets of Summer* is full of deft caricature and amiable cheek. Who says twelve-tone music can't discombobulate the funny bone?"

And Udo Kasemets talks about *Place of Meeting*, which was commissioned by the Toronto Mendelssohn Choir for Centennial Year, in this way: "He pays tribute, half-ironically, half-affectionately, to his country and his people. Drawing on some Ivesian means (independent ensembles led by two conductors, juxtaposition of art and popular music idioms, episodes of "musical realism", etc.), yet maintaining his own mode of speech, he paints a most vivid picture of the physical, emotional and intellectual life of present-day Canada."

A later collaboration with Reaney was *Canada Dash, Canada Dot.* "The Line Across" section is a quick dash from coast to coast and includes a collage of sounds characteristic of each area the "dash" runs past. In the second section, "The Line Up and Down", the listener travels up Yonge Street from the cacophony of Toronto, through the suburbs into the farms and finishes at the village of Sharon's quiet reality. *Canada Dot,* completed in 1967, darts here and there in the grid so formed.

Sharon is a nodal point for Beckwith spiritually and musically. It is a place he takes students as well. What many feel to be his most beautiful piece of music is *Sharon Fragments.* It is really one of his instrumental pieces, in a sense, because it depends for its text on fragments written by David Willson in journals and hymns and these fragments are apportioned among the voices, which take on the character of instruments rather than dramatic personalities as in his collaborations. This piece is completely Beckwith's own since he compiled the text himself.

Another instrumental piece that is also considered to be Beckwith at his best is *Circle, With Tangents,* a Centennial Year commission from the Vancouver Festival Society. Writing about the collage texture of this piece with its recurring, raw elements of "pitch patterns drawn from two interrelated note series, glides, note-clusters, rhythm patterns of long-short, long-short, common to marches and to some strutting forms of early jazz", Beckwith mentions the two important influences on his work. "If the grandfather of this sort of composition is Charles Ives, the godmothers of this particular work are a series of music-and-poetry 'collages' written in collaboration with James Reaney, which have occupied me quite a lot over the last years. *Circle, With Tangents* is my first attempt at applying collage procedures to a purely instrumental medium."

Of the composers writing today, Beckwith is generally considered the most "Canadian" in his approach. This doesn't mean that he is trying for a Canadian "sound", but that his environment influences whatever he does. "I believe in the importance of environment, local colour, 'accent'. Music, no less than its sister arts, achieves universality at least partly through loving care and attention paid to these things. (Look at Bach, Chopin, Ives.) All this is *not* simply the old advocacy of 'folk' all over again; nor does it rule out the necessity for awareness of international technical and linguistic advances."

Such a Canadian expression, he feels, occurs "by seepage". Canada's artists have "to argue for a distinct identity", and there is "a lot of untapped possibility in the Canadian experience".

Similarly, in today's art world, he believes the emphasis on Eastern mysticism is often misdirected. He agrees with modern composer Luciano Berio, who, replying to a student questioner on a visit to Toronto, mentioned that the new generation's affinities with Oriental philosophy are interesting and educational, and everyone should be aware of them — but not allow them to change one's nature. Beckwith says: "You can't turn into a Buddhist if you are a Canadian. It's presumptuous to remake sixty generations of Western culture overnight, or for that matter, to incorporate sixty generations of Oriental culture."

He recalls, ironically, seeing the Peking Opera perform. The Chinese themselves seemed most proud of rendering pieces of fake Khatchatourian while making excuses for, "one old guy who played drums and sang in the traditional manner who was, for me, the highlight of the whole thing."

Typically, the course John Beckwith continues to teach at the University of Toronto is one he established himself. Called "Music of North America" it traces the growth of music on this continent from early Indian music to the present. Two of his own compositions that are the result of his studies in this field are *The Sun Dance* and *Five Songs. The Sun Dance* has words adapted in part from Plains Cree texts and is set for chorus, organ, male speaker, six soloists, four vocal sub-groups, and percussion instruments of unusual kinds, including among others a deep tom-tom, a gourd rattle, sleigh-bells, a large cowbell, a large hand-drum and a wind harp.

Five Songs is an arrangement for alto voice and piano based on Canadian folk songs: two from Quebec, one from the Atlantic Provinces and two from the Prairies (represented by a Ukrainian and a Lithuanian song). These were finished in early 1970. (A companion set, *Four Love Songs*, for baritone voice, was also published in 1970.)

Since 1965 he has been working on other pieces including *The Shivaree*, another opera in collaboration with James Reaney. After being appointed Dean of the Faculty of Music in 1971, John Beckwith also had the time-consuming duties of that office. He resents the amount they cut into his creative energies; but administration, he says, ''is too important to be left to the hucksters.''

Fortunately for the Faculty, Beckwith understands and appreciates all forms of music. In 1965 he was given a Canada Council senior award to study electronic music. That same year he was able to begin *The Shivaree*.

In 1961 he had this to say about his music. ''As to my style and method of composing, I lean as much as anything towards the French Neoclassic school; though I have also been influenced, I believe, by such Americans as Thomson and Copland.'' At the end of the sixties, in answer to the question, ''What interests you most in contemporary trends in music?'' he wrote to Keith MacMillan at the Canadian Music Centre: ''The effects, direct and indirect, of electronic composition. I notice that whereas in the forties and fifties we used to call for 'clarity', we seem to be more interested now in dealing with a certain confusion, a certain cloudiness; clarity has already a period feel to it. The confusion is the result of several breakdowns: between 'pop' and 'serious', between Western and Oriental, between musical sound and noise, between music and the other arts, and so on. Naturally, to someone with a creative bent all this is tremendously vital and stimulating. . . .''

And what of those young Canadian composers and musicians to whom much of his life has been dedicated? He would wish to impart to them "a sense of the fun, the sheer joy of music, and at the same time a sense of its deep magical seriousness. A sense also of the vastness of the repertoire of what we can call 'good music', of all kinds, and a sense too of critical tolerance for everything in that repertoire."

The father of four children (Lawrence was added to Robin-Jane, Jonathan and Simon in December 1962), John Beckwith obviously remains energetically in the midstream of what is happening, not only in music but in society in general. As he does in his own work, Dean Beckwith tries to make students examine their own motives and the materials of their compositions in such a way that they can raise questions which will lead to their own development. How can a composition be more adventurous? More daring?

Just as David Willson must have sat pondering the large questions of his time and place, in his brilliantly-illuminated study at Sharon, so John Beckwith may often be seen – by students and visitors arriving at his glass-walled office in the Edward Johnson Building – sitting at a round teak table, catching a precious moment to contemplate, or to put finishing touches to a piece of work.

Sharon appeals to him because it was a place where people were "making and doing". As well as its barrel-organ, possibly the first to be built in Canada, and its famous girls' choir, it probably had the first non-military band and first music instruction program in Ontario. Creativity. Artistic vitality. John Beckwith says about the future, "I'm ready to accept every new venture on its individual merits – wishing fervently for the same minimum acceptance myself."

suspended sounds of
norma beecroft

At least the forties things her mother wore – she'd been an actress – had elegance, flair . . . puffed shoulders, wide collars. . . . Norma flung the twentieth, last, dullest coat around her. These were winter lines. *All the wrong length . . . for one thing . . . and beltless. . . .* Nothing to cinch about her thin waist to suggest a line. . . . *How the hell can you make a thing like that look good?* It was hot work to be doing in August, in a stuffy warehouse showroom on Spadina Avenue, in the sweatshop garment district of Toronto. *Suits, they weren't so bad. At least they realized you needed more time to change into them.*

The buyers were sweating in the heat as well. They didn't say much, just looked the numbers over, scratched notes on little pads taken out of their inside jacket pockets as soon as they sat down to take a look at the new lines. *No 16: Might go over in the suburbs.*

It wasn't exactly the romantic life Dorothy Fleming's model school had seemed to hold out for her. But it left her time to study and it brought in enough to pay for her piano lessons and support herself in the grimy city she'd been in now for . . . *what? . . . nearly two and a half years?*

You meet the oddest people in the strangest places. When she'd first come to the city, leaving behind the old house in Whitby, lying about her age, she'd worked as a file clerk for Manufacturers Life. First day on the job, walking to her small desk in the vast room. . . . Wow! Just like something out of Kafka! The white noise of typewriters banging out policies had stunned her. Worse than a fieldful of crickets. Then being called in to see Mr Laurie, sitting high over it all like an orchestra conductor. ''A musician? Let me tell you about my son.''

He, himself, had been a string player, a violinist with an orchestra in England. Too many years ago. Ron, his son, was a well-known Toronto cellist. Behind the desk in his quieter locale he spoke to her about the musical life. Talented as she was, she should continue working at it. *You have to do what you really want to do, no matter what it takes to do it.*

At home, using what music she'd learned as a choir singer,

she'd taught herself how to play the piano. Earlier her parents had decided she should play the violin. She hadn't been able to stand the scratchy sounds, had given it up. Her parents were both musically trained. Even her father. Or especially her father. Dedicating his life to becoming a concert pianist and a composer, he had abandoned formal education and was all set to meet George Gershwin in New York when a terrible accident with machinery he was using caused him to lose three fingers from his left hand. All during her childhood, including the Second World War, her father had played with dancebands in the evening, after the day spent working in his machine shop or in her grandfather's lumberyard. He loved to sit and play his favourite melodies – Debussy, Chopin and Cole Porter – faking the bass amazingly well with his damaged hand.

But now she was on her own. She made her own decisions and paid her own way. Life was completely different from a few years ago. It would never be the same as before in the comfortable closeness of her family. Since her parents had separated, the rest of the family seemed to be breaking apart also. Her elder sister Jane, the poetic, artistic one, had joined her mother in Toronto and stayed with her for a few years while getting art training at Danforth Technical School. Shortly after Norma too came to Toronto, Jane went to work in advertising promotion.

There was never any one time, she'd explain to Mr Laurie, that her whole life hadn't been blanketed in the sound of music. It just seemed the natural thing for her. As children, she and Jane had sung in the choir, alto, the difficult part. Learning to sight-read had come to her as naturally as swimming or bicycle-riding came to other children. Playing the piano came casually too – as boys learn by themselves to play baseball or hockey.

For two years she'd studied piano regularly, while working at the insurance company and having long chats with Mr Laurie. She had soon decided she needed more time for the music. And, in a naïve way, she had begun to compose.

Every quiet moment she could gather, she would sit in her

room and try to notate her own inventions. Her mother, aware of her problem, suggested Norma go to Sterndale Bennett's acting school (she herself being a member of the University Women's Alumnae Dramatic Club).

Norma was certainly good-looking enough – dramatic black hair, definite features on a wide, elegant face. In fact, she had half-thought of a music performing career herself since she had an excellent, rich singing voice and a quick intelligence. But one awful experience at school had made her sure of failure in those kinds of careers, and there had grown in her what proved to be a lifelong nervousness at public gatherings.

She'd been asked by her high-school teachers in Whitby to put her name up as a candidate for literary president of the arts club, which held annual elections. She was in Grade Eleven. Always the youngest in her class because she had skipped grades, she was tormented by the idea of the speech. Finally, on stage, bewildered with nervousness, she'd forgotten completely what she was supposed to say. Everybody was staring at her. She was supposed to be selling herself. But what was there to sell? She heard her own voice like a stranger's, stumbling through a few silly sentences in the awful silence. Then she'd fled from the podium, unable to finish. She didn't get the presidency.

This modelling career, then, seemed at first to be the solution. But she was getting busier; and besides, long fingernails being the fashion, she was constantly being chided for cutting them so she could continue to play. There were other problems, too – many of which kept getting in the way of her dedication to the world of sounds.

At this time she was trying to compose, as well as play. A whole new career by itself going on inside her head, unseen and unrecognized. She'd catch a phrase or a musical blend in her mind, be unable to work it out, and at the end of a tough day, be unable to recapture it. Reading music was easy. But getting it out of her head onto paper was proving difficult. She needed help to get over that, as well as more of a background in composition theory.

82 soundprints

One of the salesmen she'd come to know walked over to chat with her as the show ended. He was a kind, cheerful person, always joking.

"How's it going, Norma?"

"Well. I've got a few things written, you know. But it's tougher than I'd thought. What I really need is a good teacher. Someone to get me over the hump."

"Hey! Why didn't you let me know before? There's this great guy I know. Good teacher. Teaches at the Conservatory. Weinzweig. You've never heard of him? John Weinzweig."

It was near the fall of 1952. Norma phoned John Weinzweig and went down to see him. It was in the old Royal Conservatory of Music building, which had been converted from use as a college at the University of Toronto. (Later it was torn down for a parking lot.) John Weinzweig sat in his small office. He greeted her. She sat down. She gave him some scores she'd been trying to work on. He looked at them a minute. They were naïve, simple, but unusual for a person almost completely uneducated in music theory. On the phone she'd struck him as an intelligent person. She was eighteen. On the threshold of her adult life. At the stage when her life could take a hundred different directions.

"Well, Norma. So you want to be a composer."

"Yes, Mr Weinzweig."

"What for?"

She grinned. He smiled. They both knew it was because they were lost in the enchanted maze of sound. Like himself, Norma could think of little else.

Born in 1934 in Oshawa, Norma, as many others her age, remembers the tag-end of the Depression. A perfectionist, a man of deep seriousness and concentration, Norma's father had been working in her grandfather's lumberyard until 1929, at which point he had begun to build cabin cruisers. In 1934, when Norma was born, he was using his large range of mechanical and inventive skills as an expert in wood fashioning at the Sackville Shops' furniture design factory. Later, he became a die designer at DeHavilland Aircraft, and under the auspices of the

RCAF and the provincial Department of Education involved himself with placement and training programs during the war years, since he could not be accepted for active service.

The family house was in Whitby where her grandfather lived, but her parents soon moved to Collingwood, the summer and ski resort on Georgian Bay, where the family of five grew up. Besides Norma's elder sister Jane, there was a younger brother Eric, who later worked at the CBC, went on to the National Film Board, and England. Younger still was Charles, who wanted to be an engineer; and the youngest, Caroline, who unlike the others in the family settled for a more conventional life in Whitby with a husband and children.

Of the two older sisters, Jane was more wilful, emotional and independent. Norma was less of a handful, content to let her elder sister lead the way. She tended to be passive and flexible; although once, when she was about ten, a fit of temper made her smash a window pane.

In Collingwood, and later back at Whitby, her father continued to operate his own small machine shop. He was an inventor and craftsman, and Norma, especially, enjoyed helping him and watching him experiment. He was, at one time, experimenting with electronic equipment and came up with the idea of using magnetic tape for sound reproduction, which many others were working on at the same time. He never patented his method, and very soon afterwards the concept transformed communication. Norma was always fascinated by the things he did, but she insists now that she had never really acquired anything more than the rudimentary skills.

One of the distinguishing marks of Norma Beecroft's compositions is her use of the new electronic media. "I don't find electronics unnatural — I've grown with them — yet I prefer electronic sound in combination with instruments and voices. We like the human sounds because they have warmth, character, individual qualities. The combination of these qualities and both abstract and concrete tapes, for particular communicative purposes, is what fascinates me and will probably continue to do so." Perhaps a technical medium satisfies her need to communicate

84 soundprints

without the danger of the personal confrontation of an acting career. Unlike many other practitioners of "media music", Norma does feel that need to communicate. "I think composers feel this more urgently than they have for many years. I disagree categorically with composers who are not interested in communication."

She was fortunate to have excellent music teachers at her school, who taught her all the basics of choral singing, and encouraged her talent. She and Jane would practise their alto harmonies for hours together, sometimes sunning on the balcony, their voices going out over the grinding and hammering sounds from their father's shop. At other times they'd be on the balcony listening to that marvel, radio, especially *Escape with Me*. "It was a bit sticky I guess by our modern standards, but it had the root of the Romantic in it and was full of music by Debussy and Ravel. . . . I gained an affection for Debussy that has never left me and that has probably been basic to my personal, musical aesthetic."

The family was a close one, at least as far as the children were concerned. Norma's beautiful, eccentric mother kept busy pursuing her dramatic interests. A talented woman in many ways, she had studied the piano, singing, and ballet before marrying Norma's father, Julian. Norma's grandfather had been an ardent United Church supporter during its formation and his sister had been a missionary. (The choir the two girls would later sing for in Whitby was United Church too.) Jane took religion more seriously than Norma. Norma had always tended to be the one who helped out her father in the shop and busied herself with things round the house.

But the closeness must have been partly an illusion. When Norma was twelve, Jane fourteen, and Caroline, the youngest, only two or so, their mother and father separated. The children went to live with their father at their grandfather's place in Whitby. Grandfather Beecroft was alone now because his wife had died in 1945.

The split affected them all, but most of all Jane. Converted to Catholicism at about age eighteen, she decided some years later to enter religious orders – becoming Sister Ignatia. She stayed seven years, and then, two years before taking her final vows, decided to renounce that life to become a poet and artist.

At Whitby their father was still experimenting in his spare time. At that time he was making small parts under contract for the Wayne Pump Company. All the children helped. Norma would start the brass lathe and watch fine, gold spirals curl off the blurred, speeding stock as she guided the turning point with her steady, young hand. She also worked the drill press.

At age sixteen Norma followed Jane's example and left for Toronto. None of the children went through university. Their father was self-educated, self-employed, and didn't really see the value of it. It just wasn't part of the family's idea of what was necessary in life. Besides, there would have been a financial problem. Norma, for instance, never felt comfortable at the thought of asking for formal piano lessons until she was working and could pay for them herself.

Studying under John Weinzweig at the Conservatory inspired her to stop modelling. One day she had begun studying the difficult techniques of counterpoint. The amazing experience of suddenly producing at the same time two independent yet related ''lines'' of music, that contrasted, complemented, or conversed with each other, opened her ears to the possibilities that lay beyond purely vertical harmonies. Her own compositions took a corresponding leap forward.

At the Conservatory she met others like herself: Murray Schafer, Bruce Mather, Irving Glick, Rudi Van Dijk. Once Murray Schafer said he felt he could have done any number of things equally well. *Why was it, somehow, they had been chosen in the order of things to be COMPOSERS for heaven's sake?* All the noted composers in Canada could have done many other things. And many, including Murray Schafer and John Beckwith, have done just that by expanding their natural talents into other areas where they have become well known for innovation. Norma, herself, would soon move into the CBC and contribute, over the many years she stayed, a creative legacy to the organization, especially in CBC radio music programming and documentaries.

Unlike her fellow students at the Conservatory, Norma did not have a formal education in music. During her years studying with John Weinzweig she wrote some of the Conservatory exams, but decided, with the assent of her teacher, that most would be a waste of time for her if she wanted to apply herself to composition.

In 1954 CBC television was still in its infancy, just entering a golden period that spawned many extraordinary artists and innovators. Norma began working there as a script assistant, having responsibilities for as many as three programs a week — a phenomenal amount by today's standards. From that experience she learned how to work to deadlines, something she is now trying to work out of, because she feels, to be truly excellent, work must sometimes grow slowly and not be forced.

The vitality of the Corporation in those days depended on two things. One was the necessity for live performance since videotape was not yet in common use. The other was the experimental nature of the new medium, in which there were as yet no ''experts''. Thus, people with many different kinds of talent came with their particular vision and added to the stock of what was possible. Norma was one of the youngest of this group — applying her musical expertise and powers of independent judgement to her programming over the years, while drawing on her growing technical knowledge of the medium in her own artistic development as a composer. Composing still took second place — at night or on weekends.

By now she was taking lessons in John Weinzweig's house on Belgravia Avenue. Her fascination with counterpoint continued and she began writing her own music under his direction. Thursday nights she would often arrive early for supper with the Weinzweigs and she became firm friends with them. This close pupil-teacher relationship continued for nearly seven years until 1959.

Through John Weinzweig she became concerned about Canadian music and its future. Norma became president of the Concert Committee of the Canadian Music Associates. As it turned out, she was its final president, since the organization was on the point of breaking up, for lack of funds and public interest. But before it did so, Norma met Aaron Copland, who suggested she might apply to study at Tanglewood, the Berkshire Music Centre, which, among other things, is the summer home of the Boston Symphony Orchestra. She sent in a clutch of manuscripts she'd composed by then, and on the strength of these she was accepted. This was the summer of 1958. It was an important scholarship since it gave her the confidence to realize she could be, in time, a composer capable of doing work at an international level. She had a public, however small.

It wasn't the first scholarship she had won. Earlier the Conservatory had given her one to continue her studies with John Weinzweig. Besides helping her economically, that previous scholarship had had another effect, accidental but important to Norma's developing interest in ''line''. Part of the condition of the scholarship was that she had to learn to play another instrument. She had chosen the flute. (She is still a competent, though ''rusty'', player.) The experience opened up a whole range of music that went beyond the dense ''vertical harmony'' that seems so natural to the piano. She began to ''feel'' line – to integrate it into her compositional repertoire – rather than simply to ''know'' it.

Now Tanglewood kept her busy. Every hour, it seemed, there was a concert of one kind or another. It was Norma's first experience with what was happening in the international music world at that time. She had little experience with the twelve-tone system of Schoenberg and what she heard at Tanglewood was even more modernistic. The notions of music which constituted her basic philosophy were assaulted so violently that the shock stayed with her for many years, until she was able to integrate these new ideas into her sensibility.

Attempting to write a chamber piece for her teacher, Lukas Foss, she found everything she was doing seemed derivative. Hearing a Mozart concert would lead to her producing phrases that sounded Mozartian. When she listened to Hindemith her work became Hindemithian. Foss was sympathetic. *Hear everything. Understand all you can. Your own voice will grow in its own time.* Norma was encouraged.

In her class with Lukas Foss were people like Zubin Mehta, the young Indian conductor whose career took him to Montreal and Los Angeles; Claudio Abbado, another important conductor; and composers from all over the world. (Norma reads about them now in music news, except for those who seem to have disappeared from sight altogether.) Discussions with these class-mates convinced her she should go to Europe. But how would she get there? Would the CBC give her time off? They'd already done so for Tanglewood. What if she went to Europe, came back and had to start all over again? And where would the money come from?

She applied to the Canada Council. It refused her. The Coun-cil wasn't prepared to give grants to untried talents, no matter what high recommendations it had. Well. That was that. She started back to Toronto. When she arrived a letter was waiting for her. It was from a legal firm. She opened it. A great uncle who had been in hospital for ten years had died recently. His estate was being divided among the members of her family. The amount was much larger than expected. The will wouldn't be probated for a considerable time, but Norma managed to bor-row on the strength of it. She was ready to take her chances abroad.

Her brother, Eric, left for England about the same time. After a short stay in London ("It took me years to like London. All the worst in architecture.") she arrived in Paris. "The architecture was overwhelming." But the fabled unfriendliness of that city (to its first-time visitors) soon affected her. Since she was travel-ling alone she spoke only to ticket collectors and desk clerks. She understood little of what went on around her. Soon, a strange emptiness seemed to come into her life. She had ar-ranged to study in Rome at the St Cecilia academy with the composer Goffredo Petrassi, but that was still months ahead.

Fleeing the loneliness, she travelled almost aimlessly. At least travelling had a pattern to it. Buses, railway stations, travellers' cafés, small hotels – these things became familiar, predictable and manageable. Gradually the beauties of Europe poked like

norma beecroft 89

daffodils over the grimy confusion of her everyday life. She was getting over her culture shock at last. After a short stay in Munich she arrived in Vienna and met some friends there, people from Toronto, and also Zubin Mehta, her good friend from Tanglewood days. It was festival time for a little while until the group went their various ways and she set out for Rome in high spirits.

She had arranged to stay with an Italian family in Rome, since she felt that was the quickest way to learn the language and customs. Unfortunately the family was undergoing its own problems and the frequent, hysterical outbursts disturbed her enormously. She had to find a place to stay where she'd be able to study in quiet.

Luckily, she had written down the address of Dr Chevalier, a Canadian who worked in the Immigration Department of the Canadian Embassy there. She'd never met him, but by chance she'd been given his name by two doctors from Canada whom she and Eric had met in a London pub months before. Hearing that the young composer was alone in the city he managed to arrange a "pied à terre" for her and made sure she was introduced to all his official contacts. A favour that made things much easier for her.

Her "pied à terre" was a small apartment inside a larger apartment. It consisted more or less of one room with a two-burner stove in it, but elegantly furnished. It was the kind of place usually used for other purposes. That gave it a somewhat titillating air, which Norma found amusing.

Her "landlord" came to the door. He was very tall and strong and reached out a huge hand. He was dressed in a suit, but his identity was unmistakable. It was – Tarzan!

"And here" said Tarzan, "is my wife, Eva."

Norma got to know Lex Barker and Eva Gabor quite well. Well enough to have the occasional disagreement with her landlord, as most long-standing tenants do. Their lives were quite different from hers, naturally, but she enjoyed the excitement of living there, especially as it was close to the famous Via Veneto, hangout of filmstars, artists and expensive ladies.

Suddenly Norma felt secure and settled. She had begun to find herself again. Perhaps a different self, but her eagerness to learn composing was stronger than ever.

In a very short time she was able to arrange an interview with Goffredo Petrassi. Fortunately, her ear for languages was very good. In about two weeks she could make herself understood, although Goffredo spoke very little English. She had written him before, and that, plus what they managed to convey to each other, convinced both of them that their basic musical aesthetic was similar.

"One thing," said Goffredo, "you must learn Italian to be in the class."

Norma did just that. Like many musical people she discovered she had a real language skill. In less than two months she was almost fluent, able to discuss quite esoteric musical concepts.

That Christmas, her brother Eric arrived from England. Norma cooked a Canadian-style Christmas dinner — using Tarzan's large stove for the turkey and preparing the rest of the meal by juggling pots on her two-burner. Invited were a mixed bag of new friends she'd made during her short stay.

Her "Corso di Perfezionamento" consisted of a great deal of score analysing, particularly of contemporary music — music by such twentieth-century masters as Hindemith, Stravinsky, Bartok. Goffredo Petrassi, as many other composers, was going through his own transitional period.

As in all the arts, new technology had opened up whole new worlds of exploration and had changed many of the accepted, traditional notions of form. It was a troubling time for many, deciding where lay the line between gimmickry and sincere exploration. Many reacted strongly and totally rejected the new expressions. Others did the opposite. Norma's own writing consisted mainly of exercises. Although she never thought of them as "compositions", they gave her a great deal of writing experience.

At the end of the five-month semester Norma left for Darmstadt, in Germany, to find out about the new forms for herself from Bruno Maderna. The shock she had experienced at Tanglewood was still unresolved. Her first day at Darmstadt, Norma opened the door by mistake on a class being given by David Tudor, an exponent of John Cage's ideas on sound education. The class was studying the various sounds made by a chair being scraped across the floor. After the "traditional" teaching methods at the academy in Italy, this was revolutionary. What was "sound" and what was music?

But by listening to just-written music by serious exponents of the avant-garde, Norma began to understand what was going on. She was particularly excited to hear the electronic pieces. Much of this kind of music, in a very much watered-down form, is what we have now become used to as background music on television or in films.

After Darmstadt and Bruno Maderna's lectures Norma felt she had a grasp of the techniques. But how to put it together and use it? She began work on her *Tre Pezzi Brevi* (three little pieces) for flute and harp. It would be performed in Darmstadt the following summer. (Severino Gazzelloni, who had inspired her to go to study in Darmstadt, wanted to use it for a performance in Palermo but needed a version for guitar since a harpist was unavailable. And eventually she would write yet another version, for flute and piano.)

Visiting her brother in London, Norma kept working on the piece and trying to decide whether or not to return to Rome. Now that she was beginning to understand the new music, what was the point of putting in a difficult, graduating year at St Cecilia's? But Norma felt she still needed to get that musical background. She had begun to realize that everything a composer hears or learns affects the quality of what she writes. She had started the course. She would finish it.

It was a tough year. The most difficult part was writing a detailed analysis of the opera *Don Giovanni* – in Italian! Writing in the language was a lot more difficult than speaking it. Nevertheless, Norma scored nine out of a possible ten points to graduate with the highest marks. In February 1961, also as part of her final exams, she wrote the composition *Improvvisazioni Concertanti No. 1.*

That summer she followed Bruno Maderna to Devon, England to continue her studies in electronic music and Maderna's technique, based on a system of permutations and combinations of the twelve-tone row (or whatever other sound conventions the composer may circumscribe for herself). The system, though fascinatingly mathematical, was not rigid in application. Norma enjoys "colour" in music and will always change her electronic compositions to introduce intuitive "ear" responses. She also works only rarely with sine (pure) sounds or other electronic waveforms such as sawtooth, pulse, or triangular; she prefers to manipulate sounds electronically which have been recorded through a microphone (a method technically known as "Musique Concrète").

The awaited Darmstadt performance of her *Tre Pezzi Brevi* took place on August 31, 1961 as part of the first Studiokonzert of the Internationalen Ferienkurse für Neue Musik. It was a long weekend for Norma. Finally the papers arrived — the *Darmstädter Echo* and the *Darmstädter Tagblatt*. Her name flashed at her in the midst of the review in the *Echo*. Carefully, translating the German, she read, "Norma Beecroft shows respect for uncomplicated sound, without losing herself in effects which flute and harp could offer — a work acclaimed justly and with animation." Then, in the *Tagblatt:* "The composer Norma Beecroft from Canada wanted to write experimental new music. In her three short pieces for flute and harp she offers impressionistic, uncommon sonorities, engaging melodic phrases, delicate blendings, almost free from dissonances. A contribution pleasant to hear, and one which rises above the average. . . . "A success. There was no doubt about what would be her lifework now. Another review came in the *Mannheimer Morgen* a few days later: admiring like the others, it remarked that Norma Beecroft "goes beyond the routine arrangement of material with compelling logic and delicate mood poetry. . . . "

Her second year at St Cecilia's had been financed partly by a small Canada Council grant. What should she do now? She had learned to enjoy Italy. She also wanted to continue advanced work. A modest scholarship donated by the Italian Foreign

Ministry made that possible. But her judgement seemed to be clouded at this time by tiredness and a series of migraine headaches.

She stayed in Italy to think things over. She'd been given pills by a friend for her headaches. These were supposed to be very effective, but the pain continued. Doctors she went to ascribed it to her artistic personality and prescribed other pain-killers. Things got no better.

Looking at her suddenly-aged face in the mirror, Norma observed a small blemish. It never seemed to heal up. By now frightened and on the point of collapse, one morning she went to Dr Chevalier once again, who quickly referred her to a specialist.

In no time she was in the intensive care unit of a hospital. What was wrong with her? The doctors weren't sure. But her spleen was enormously enlarged and her blood contained practically no white cells – those which heal wounds and resist infection. The slightest infection – even a cold – and she would be dead.

They suspected leukemia. She lay watching transfusion bottles empty imperceptibly, listening to empty corridors echoing with nurses' voices and the clatter of equipment. The festival seemed almost over. She felt drained and empty – a discarded wine-bottle.

They had been up all night running tests. The doctor came in. He told her he'd found the problem – an allergy to the substance commonly used in the pain-killers of various kinds she'd been taking. A vicious cycle had been established. Perhaps its effects were permanent. He couldn't say. A nurse gave her a massive injection of cortisone.

One morning several days later she woke feeling stronger. Yes. The cortisone was working. The transformation was astonishing. Her brother had come from England to see her. Her spirits rose with her increasing good health. Now she could begin to think clearly. Europe had matured her. She'd learned many things. Even, perhaps, how to face death. But Canada, home, was where she wanted to go, now, while her life-senses were so

94 soundprints

acute and she was impatient to begin work again.

Earlier, newspaper editor Nathan Cohen had wanted her to write a review of the Venice Music Festival and she'd been unable to do this. But it was a sign that "back home" people were beginning to know about her and her work. She'd go back there for a time to do some composing and renew acquaintanceships, then return, if she felt like it.

But landing in July 1962 in Canada she was astounded at the country's beauty. After the crowded aridity of southern Italy everything seemed so incredibly green. The greenness made her stay. The CBC took her back. It was the old story. Her Darmstadt notices had given her respectability. *You have to leave to get recognized.* Quickly she was promoted to an administrative position – first as talent relations officer, then later as program organizer in the Music Department.

She went back to Italy for a short while only in 1963. The associations were too much for her. It was not until her own piece, *Rasas,* was performed as part of the Canadian Music Concert given in May 1972 that she returned. This time the ghosts had left her and she fell in love with Italy all over again.

She had been offered scholarships to study electronic music in Europe (in Rome and Cologne) but turned them down. Instead she attended a seminar at the Faculty of Music of the University of Toronto. She was home again and composing well. In 1962 just before her return, she wrote *Contrasts for Six Performers* for oboe, viola, xylorimba, vibraphone, percussion and harp – a most original treatment with unusual instrumentation. This was followed shortly by *From Dreams of Brass.* This cantata for voices and orchestra was based on a long poem of her sister Jane's, written while Norma was ill. In this piece electronic music is used as an extension of the orchestra and as a link between narrator, soprano and chorus. Jane describes her text as a "discussion of love as it exists and acts in the universe, but particularly concerning Man, who, unlike the rest of the universe, is free to reject or accept love (God), bringing upon himself either utter aloneness, or a beatitude without bounds."

Irving Glick, composer and critic, was among those who were

"impressed by its musicality, its dramatic nature. To write a work of sixteen minutes' duration for such large forces is no mean feat. The style of the music is, of course, avant-garde, pointillistic, but it is a work that people will be able to recognize for its strong musicality."

Like many modern composers, Norma has had her share of mixed notices from critics who are unable to convince themselves that modern — especially electronic — music is a worthwhile artform. But even in those instances words such as "softness", "delicacy", and "musicality" are frequently used to describe her treatment of the materials she uses. But the patronizing attitude of many critics to modern work is just one problem which the innovative composer has to deal with. Another difficulty, and a more basic one, is obtaining the proper equipment. Things are much better now, at least in Toronto, since the electronic music studio of the Faculty of Music acquired a serial structure generator (sometimes called an electronic composing machine). But in 1963 while working on *From Dreams of Brass,* Norma had to obtain leave of absence from the CBC to go to Columbia University for the right equipment and the services of a "Tone Meister".

The work was originally requested by Walter Susskind, who wanted an electronic tape and orchestra work. At Columbia it was easier for Norma because of the Tone Meister, a technical person who assists the composer to produce the combinations of sounds she wants. These days Norma works at the University of Toronto's electronic music studio and frequently observes young students who, she says, have no problem with the equipment at all, taking it for granted in the same way she takes for granted electric appliances which her grandmother could never get used to.

Nineteen sixty-seven, Centennial Year, gave a great impetus to composing. There was money available for commissions, and the composers found themselves hard at work. Norma's production that year had a wide range. It included *Undersea Fantasy,* a twenty-minute electronic piece for the Expo puppet show repertoire, two works using Leonard Cohen poetry *(Elegy* and *Two*

Went to Sleep), and a choral work for Waterloo Lutheran University, *The Living Flame of Love.*

The choral work presented Norma with the greatest problems. Part of a series originated by Walter Kemp, in which all works performed would be published, the work had to be done with the limitations of a student choir in mind. Norma's solution was a typically original one. She would write a modern piece which would reflect the austere tonality of early Spanish church music. The text she chose for it was from St John of the Cross, which Norma translated from the Spanish herself with some assistance from her sister. This work was recorded in 1972 by the Festival Singers of Canada under the direction of Elmer Iseler.

Two Went to Sleep and *Elegy* combine those elements which Norma seems most to enjoy: voice, flute and electronic music. Two of her most successful pieces, they have been described by the critics as ''jewels''. Norma selected the text for *Elegy* from Cohen's *Let Us Compare Mythologies.* ''In the process of writing this song, I noticed all the accidentals I was writing indicated that the piece is in the key of E flat – my very first diatonic song!''

Two Went to Sleep, from Cohen's *Parasites of Heaven,* seemed to suggest a more contemporary treatment. She read the words over and over, mulling phrases and sentences in her mind during long walks. It struck her that the ''dream'' theme of the poem and its echoing rhymes had qualities she could put into music. Rather than simply having the poem ''sung'', what if she transformed its words into her own medium entirely? *In other words, create a musical event from the poem rather than merely colouring the poem with music.* Mary Morrison, one of Canada's most talented singers of contemporary music, read the poem onto tape, rather than singing it. She did this several times with different intonations and emphasis. Also put onto tape was the opening passage of the flute score. These sounds Norma took and transformed electronically, by filtering, reverberation, speed changes, reversal of the original, montage, and so on. She then spliced them together in a predetermined order. This stereo tape now forms part of the score for spoken voice, flute, percussion and stereo tape. The hallucinatory effect of the whole with its strange, echoing suggestions and its inner contrasts is a complete transformation of Cohen's original inspiration into purely musical terms.

All this work in one year left Norma exhausted. In 1968 she was at work on only one work, commissioned by the Société de Musique contemporaine du Québec. But it was a substantial work for flute, harp, violin, viola, cello, percussion and piano, which she did not complete until 1969.

That year, 1968, was important in other ways as well. She married John Wright, a dark-haired, good-looking, energetic lawyer, who was also a graduate of the Royal Military College. Now, besides her CBC work there were two places she most wanted to apply her emotional energy: to her marriage and her composing. The strain brought on a succession of vicious, "cluster" migraine attacks. It was obvious what had to go. The CBC.

"People who have ordinary jobs really have no notion of the tension and emotional drain of creative work," Norma says. If the tension is not meaningfully expressed it either gets taken out on the outside world or, in Norma's case, on herself. The CBC promoted her again as she was considering her decision. But there was no hesitation. She resigned. For the first time in her life she was going to be a composer and nothing else.

Rasas, the work she completed in 1969, is the plural of "Rasa", a word used frequently in Sanskrit poetry. Difficult to translate, it means a certain kind of mood, flavour or taste. In Sanskrit philosophy there are nine basic emotions, the last being "peace". The work follows these classifications but is constructed so that the performers can adjust and improvise according to their own sense of mood and audience reaction. Thus, no two performances are alike. The flute and piano offer the lyric elements, and the functions of the other instruments are primarily textural. Violins wail, gongs sound, and above these the flute draws out lines of long, sustained notes — difficult to play — while the piano adds its own peculiar, percussive sequences.

Since 1969 Norma has tried to fight her early conditioning to work to deadlines. She also doesn't want an obsession with composing to make her lose out on certain other things in life. Life is more relaxed. She is learning when to ease up. When to give, instead of fight. "I decided quite early not to let work take absolute priority. I'm too interested in other things."

One of the things that continues to interest her is the promotion of contemporary music and of Canadian musicians. To that end she became the founding president of the New Music Concert Series. The idea for this organization grew out of conversations with Robert Aitken, who became the organization's artistic director. Norma was still titular president of the Ten Centuries Concert Series, which Murray Schafer had begun but which was now non-functioning after several successful years.

This new organization was designed to tackle difficult contemporary music, and by so doing to build an ensemble of established and younger musicians who would become familiar with a contemporary repertoire. At first the idea was to keep the organization small and voluntary, but the problems presented by that kind of structure were ones Norma felt should be avoided, if at all possible, by establishing the organization on a thoroughly professional basis right from the start. This kind of thinking persuaded the Canada Council and the Ontario Arts Council to give meaningful support, and the series began with a year of high-quality, successful productions, often attended by guest composers who would help rehearse and also conduct, as well as be on hand to explain their music to the audience.

Because she enjoys it, Norma continues to do freelance work for the CBC – creating documentaries by splicing master tapes on the comparatively simple machinery she keeps in her small, attic studio. One about Harry Somers was done this way. Her husband's study-den, lined with leather books and hung with RMC mementoes, is downstairs.

Taking a break from their work, they meet in the friendly kitchen and share a drink around its central, small bar. Norma lavishes care on an extensive plant collection at the kitchen's sunny window. The house is an old one on a quiet, tree-lined street in midtown Toronto, close to Avenue Road and the fash-

norma beecroft 99

ionable apartment houses there. Since it was too small for a separate dining room, Norma converted a sun porch at the back. The furniture is custom-crafted in a clean Jacobean style – a magnificent table with matching benches. A rose-coloured, shag broadloom gives the room a soft, delicate air which tall, pink candles emphasize.

Norma likes light. Eventually she will put a glass roof on her attic to bring in the north light. She hates the way the electronic music studio is buried in the sub-basement of the Edward Johnson Building. *No light. The air still and dead. Like descending into ancient Egyptian crypts.* She drives down there, in summer, in a bright little MG with the top down.

Constantly at work on new commissions, she tries to make her new lifestyle work out in her music by letting ideas grow and develop without forcing. Her quest is a long-range one. She is searching for a particular kind of music: ''Music with a feeling of suspended sound – and this is something I can't parcel out precisely and can't rush.''

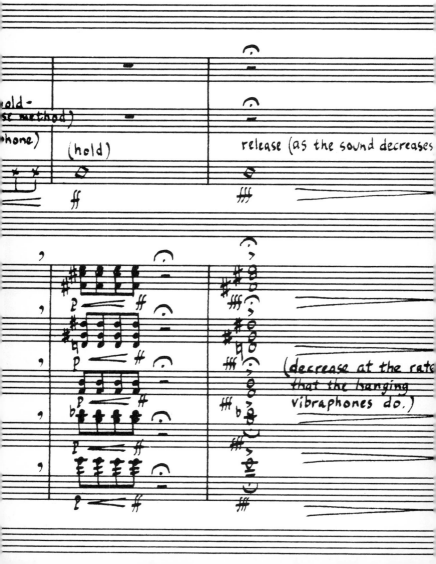

here was John, Genevieve, then Katherine. After her came Nicholas, then another boy who died very young, then Walter's brother, Teddy, and in 1933 the seventh and last Buczynski child, Walter.

From John to Walter was a span of nearly twenty-three years. Walter Buczynski was only six years old when his father died in 1940. His parents were Polish immigrants, who quietly survived by working their hearts out at one menial job after another as did so many others who arrived in Canada during the Depression. His mother became ill when her husband died. She'd never learned to speak English. For many years she lay bedridden in her room while her children grew up around her. In 1953 she died of heart failure, when Walter was not yet twenty-one.

Walter grew up in a house on Dundas Street West, in a mixed immigrant area of downtown Toronto, cluttered with traffic and small shops. When he was ten years old he saw a tiny, eight-note child's piano in a variety store. His eldest brother, John, was with him at the time. They both stared into the window. John asked what he'd like to have. "Why don't you buy me that little piano, sometime?" John promised he would – as soon as he got paid.

John was working then, as a tool- and die-maker, but not for long; an obsession was growing inside him. Genevieve was working as a domestic but planning to be married, and Katherine was staying at home to care for their invalid mother and the rest of the household. Nicholas, then nearly eighteen, had gone out to work at sixteen.

Two days after he had seen the toy piano, when Walter came home from playing ball in Alexandra Park, John said: "I got your piano. It's in the living room."

At first Walter couldn't see it. Then he realized there was a huge shape against the right-hand wall. It was a monstrous, old, upright John had bought second-hand.

The traffic helicopter beats along its morning route. Below it is the Gardiner Expressway. Accident at the Jameson Ramp.

Trailer jacknifed at Highway 27. Circling, the helicopter dips near the lakeshore. The commentator, searching for a lighter moment, announces: "Well there he is again, folks. Looks like it's going to be a fine morning — we're just going over the water-front, and we can see him out there playing away — there he goes again, the fiddler on the beach."

Walter doesn't like people saying his brother John is crazy. "You know, he lives in his own world. It's not crazy to him. I owe a lot to my brother John. Though it was through him we had a lot of grief later on. None of the family were musical except John. He played the fiddle. Still does. Threw up his job. Used to practise in his room for hours. Well. It kept up like that, you know, and he wasn't contributing anything to the family."

Walter's ambition was to be a professional third baseman. He also played hockey and football. But he didn't grow very fast. That was the problem. He liked sports. Comradeship.

In St Mary's Roman Catholic public school you either turned out a saint or a convict. Composer? Are you crazy? But school was great. Fourth-year high school. That was the best year of all. Suddenly you were communicating with the teachers on a person-to-person basis. Grown-up . . . you know? He had stayed in school because he didn't want to leave. It was the De La Salle Bond Street Catholic high school. *For Grade Thirteen you had to go to De La Salle Oaklands . . . the posh place. All those teachers looked down on kids from Bond Street, and made fun of their backgrounds. Got half the subjects . . . there . . . at Oaklands. Then got the rest at Parkdale Collegiate.* He was eighteen years old when he finished school.

One and two and . . . one and two and. . . . As Mildred Wickson put her ballet pupils through their paces he played. An accompanist, the ad had said. His first job. He was a really good sight reader. Bless the early days when he never practised. Half an hour before his teacher arrived he'd get down to his lesson. *Dirty hands . . . no time to wash them after playing ball. Thirty-six dollars clear this week. That* CAPAC *competition . . . coming up soon. One-two and one-two . . . stretch . . . stretch. . . . All those beautiful legs. . . .*

Murray Ross was Walter's first piano teacher. Then he left for the United States, and Walter began lessons with Ernest Dainty. *There was a musician! Classically trained in Vienna. Made his living teaching, and playing the organ for hockey games at Maple Leaf Gardens!* Six months later Ernest Dainty died.

Walter's next teacher was composer Godfrey Ridout, who soon sent him to study piano with Earl Moss. Walter was now at the Royal Conservatory of Music in Toronto. That was fast progress in three years. It was 1947. Veterans were returning to take up where they had left off. Small, Walter would wait for lessons — lounging unnoticed in the Conservatory lobby. That way he could watch and listen. In 1949 the Opera Company was being formed. He could hear Jon Vickers' voice go ringing and ringing through the hallways. . . .

Damn. He should have put in more practice. *The thing was, in competition, you never hit the absolute top level you could sometimes manage in practice.* How could he have slurred that note? But here was a beautiful passage. Chopin! Now he was all right, his fingers knew where to go without him, he could listen to the beautiful, almost inevitable music.

First prize . . . Walter Buczynski! He'd done it! Third time lucky. The previous two years in the CAPAC competition he had come second. Another $500 into the kitty.

Nicholas had been holding it all together for the family since brother John had fallen into the deep well of music and drowned there. But now, with the worry, Katherine had become ill. The doctor advised that John leave the household. But since he seemed unwilling, the family left him and moved into a house on Shaw Street that Nicholas bought. ("We all owe Nicky a great deal. He was the pillar of the family.")

"I remember when I was a kid about eighteen, down to my last dollar, always something came up, you know. A wedding, a funeral or a little radio show, some job was always there for me. Even now. I'm going to Europe with my family, right? Costing $1,300. Well. Yesterday, I just got a royalty check. $1,200. Had no idea it was going to be that much. Little things I did years ago they're still running now and again. Fourteen dollars here. Thirty-five dollars there. In a year or so it all adds up. I feel the good Lord has always been looking after me."

Because of his CAPAC scholarship win, Walter had to turn down a job as accompanist to the National Ballet. Instead he went to Aspen, Colorado, to study under Darius Milhaud that summer. By now, 1955, he had written a violin sonata, a piano trio and a number of songs.

Darius Milhaud would look over Walter's manuscripts, glance up, and say, "Very good." And that was all. His work was performed there as he wrote it. He wrote a string quartet, a woodwind quintet and a difficult "nonette", as he calls it – a work with many tricky time changes, which has never been performed. ("And I doubt if it ever will be. It wasn't the best, you know.")

The publication and performance opportunities for Canadian composers are all too few. His *Divertimento for Four Solo Instruments* (violin, cello, bass and clarinet), which Walter wrote in 1957 and sent to the CBC to be considered for recording, was returned TEN YEARS LATER. And five years later still it was given a world première and recorded for CBC transcription services overseas. At that point, fifteen years after its composition, Walter felt the CBC might as well have forgotten it and done something more representative and recent for the international community to listen to. His woodwind quintet also had a ten-year delay in performance.

Zbigniew Drzewiecki. There was a name to conjure with. President of the Chopin Institute in Warsaw, Poland. Another name, Marion Filar, who lived in New York. Filar had been a pupil of Drzewiecki before the War. *If you wanted to get to Poland you had to play for Filar.* Too bad he hadn't decided to do this before. Last year he'd lived in New York, studying, writing, playing — now it meant a special trip. He wrote. Filar invited him down to be heard. . . .

Filar leaned back in his chair. He was proud of his mementoes. He'd been half an hour on them already. He pointed at a signed photograph on his wall. ''Do you know who that is, my boy?''

Was it maybe himself in military uniform? Or even Drzewiecki in military uniform? Why couldn't he get down to the business at hand?

''Er, no. Who is he?''

''That's General Twining.''

Impact. Silence.

''Oh?''

''You don't know General Twining?''

''No. I mean. How the hell should I know him? I'm Canadian.''

Now he'd blown it. Filar was rising from his chair.

''Well. Well. So you'd like me to write you a letter to Zbigniew? Would you like to play now?''

Walter began. A terrible piano. Took fifteen minutes to get the feel of it. For an hour he played selections of Chopin, non-stop. It was a really bad instrument. He told Filar so. Might as well be honest since he'd blown it anyway.

But Filar kept him longer, asking about his music and his intentions. *It's a hard thing to talk to great musicians unless you're actually studying with them and getting to know them.* Walter tried his best. He always managed to talk more easily about his musical aesthetic with people in other media. *Because if another musician recognizes what you're trying to do in your work there's no sense talking about it. It's there. If they don't get it . . . well. . . .*

The Baltic Sea was shining. Think of the many famous prows that had broken this brittle water, figureheads pointed eagerly westward, searching for the place he'd come from, the place he called home. His parents, too, had crowded into a ship — an old iron one with a million rusty rivets and a frightening stink in the bilge. But they would have said, if they had been alive still, that *he* was going back home. Strange — being a mixture of two cultures. Already on the Polish boat his tongue had betrayed him. His ears he could trust. He could understand nearly everything. His mother spoke always in Polish. But he had always answered her in English, and speech came hard.

This boatful of Polish nationalists had called him Canadian. Why! He couldn't even speak the language! In Canada it had always been, *Hey Polack! Why don't you go back where you came from?*

The ramp clanged. He hefted his suitcases and went down its serrated slope into the glittering town of Gdynia. He was still rolling on his legs a little from the boat, with a sharp, nervous hunger in his stomach . . . something like being in love. . . .

Warsaw was dull. He was miserable in gloomy Warsaw. Rainy, dismal, a city splotched with war and poverty still, although it was 1959. He felt lost. All the excitement of landing at Gdynia was gone. The hotel room. Noises from the street. The unenthusiastic guide had dumped him here and left. Tomorrow he could see the Chopin Institute, find out his routine, and get lodgings of a more permanent kind. He retreated into sleep. His nose was bothering him again. Another cold coming on. He hoped it would be better in the morning. . . .

Warsaw wasn't that bad after all. That was sun through his windows. He lay suspended. Energy, strange for so early in the morning, was in him . . . nerves keyed up. He got up. Shaved. The guide appeared again. *Go. Go. Go!*

Arrangements. One thing after another. It was all falling into place. He got his bags over to the dormitory of "Academic House", the student residence. He would be studying privately with Drzewiecki for one lesson a week. *All falling into place, sun shining, Warsaw not so bad after all. Look at that Chopin Institute! Like a vast museum.*

A few more days, and he began to understand his finances. He was very well off. His Polish Government scholarship, which Drzewiecki, on Filar's recommendation, had relayed through the Polish Embassy in Toronto amounted to 2,000 zlote a month.

The average wage in Poland was only 1,400 zlote. Besides, he didn't have to pay for his lessons. The student prince!

The Chopin competition was due to start on February 22, 1960. He'd wasted too much time already. He would prepare for it and enter. First, Drzewiecki completely changed his piano technique. *Fantastic*. The improvement was amazing. He listened to his colleagues practise. They were brilliant. Technically, anyway, they were miles ahead of him. His particular quality, though, was pulling out those emotional subtleties. *Practise, practise, and you could get that brilliance in your fingers. But how to get your whole brain into them, the whole spectrum of human emotion?* That was his edge, his gift. But he should practise. *More*.

He didn't. He was finding himself. It was where his roots had been. It was Warsaw with its brilliant, sensuous, young people. *Drink. Music. Dance. Song. Beautiful women*. Where could he find eight hours a day to practise?

His composing didn't slip. He worked hours writing in the "Devil's Hole". It was a stuffy, windowless room – the Philharmonic's rehearsal room. Colds. All the time he had them. Those European bugs. And also vicious pains in his belly as he sat there concentrating, or trying to concentrate. Was that from eating or drinking the wrong things? Before the year was out, he had finished his first string trio.

When it was done he poured himself into preparing for the competition. His friends joked with him. *Ah. You Canadian. What do you know about Polish music?* Wait. he told them. *You just wait. The words will come. I'll return and I'll have the words and we'll see who puts the other down*. He grew through his nationalism and beyond it, as did Chopin's music grow so that it spoke at last to a whole world. *Music. The international language*.

He did quite well. The competition lasted three weeks. Sweat poured off him. His fingers grew slippery on the keys. In his belly, those vicious pains again. Sneezing. Always he'd been sneezing since that first dismal day. A doctor had told him his nose was all wrong. If he didn't get it fixed, it would be like that all the time. *Later. Later. . . .*

Nadia. Nadia. The name sang in his nose. *Nadia Boulanger.*
Montmartre. Montmartre. The words sang in his repaired nose.
Sacré Coeur church glittered white on top of the hill. From the
jangling sin-strip of Pigalle he descended into the Métro with
its squelching rubber wheels. Typical French invention. And everywhere there were women in blue, mouths murmuring with the
kissing romance language. *Chic. Chic.* Back to the Maison Uni-
versitaire Canadienne, its quiet lobby with the large piano, the
hum of students deep in discussions, past the secretary at her
desk, buzz buzz on her intercom, and . . . up to his room. Someone began banging out, "C'est l'aviron qui nous mène, qui nous
mène." From one nationalism into another!

He lay back thinking of what he could learn from Nadia Boulanger, the great teacher. A beautiful time. Praise be to the
Canada Council and that terse notice that had meant so much,
"We are pleased to inform you that your request for a grant to
study composition theory in Paris has been approved. . . ."

That evening he went down into the buzz of French. *Les An-*
glais were sitting apart. *Not welcome. Isn't this the Canadian*
University Centre? La révolution commence. Where did that put
him and the other Polish Canadians he had run into? Sitting at
the piano he ripped out a fast Polish mazurka. Silence at the end.
A lone clap: *Give it to them again, Walter!*

Towards the end there were no *Anglais* at all. *Le Devoir* was
everywhere. And separatist posters. A serious bunch. He gave
them their dose of mazurkas twice a day. They fought back with
silence. Music wasn't their strong point, although his own
French was good enough to argue with. All *les Anglais* had been
eased out. There were four left who could speak Polish. Some
evenings they would sit in the four corners and converse across
the room in loud Polish shouts about how they were going to
start a new country somewhere on the prairies.

At summer's end he was kicked out. He left the Cité Univer-
sitaire with its maisons from so many nations in the world. Rue
de L'Odéon, five minutes from the Latin Quarter, ten from Notre
Dame Cathedral overlooking the river. Knock! Knock! Irving Glick
came to the door. "Hi, Walter. Want to move in with us, now?"

Away from *la maison,* he began work in earnest. Learning how to work. As Hemingway had done in the same city. The Polish Institute, within walking distance of him, had a "crash" apartment, which they kept for travellers in emergencies. It was completely bare of furniture. Walter rented a piano and put it there on the bare boards. No drapes at the windows. No couch to relax on. Nothing but himself and the piano. In the afternoons he composed. In between times he studied with Nadia Boulanger. Twelve hours a day, and marvellous conversations with the Glicks in the evenings. Irving Glick taught him chess.

Nadia Boulanger had told him she didn't know yet how much talent as a performer and a composer he had. That was something for him to decide for himself; but the thing he should do was to put in as much time to develop that talent as he thought it was worth. If he felt it was only worth an hour a day, well and good; but if he thought it was worth more, then that much more should he be prepared to give to it. It was clear that she was interested in people who were dedicated. Their natural talent didn't inspire her admiration as much as how hard they were willing to work. Similarly she didn't care about the style of a piece of music as long as it had integrity.

Both in his studies as a performer and as a composer, she taught him objectivity in his work. He had to develop that capacity to hear the REAL sound, not just the sound he THOUGHT he was hearing. A particularly trying class that helped him achieve that necessary critical distance was held every Thursday morning from nine to twelve. Although Mlle Boulanger called it her group session in Keyboard Harmony, it was more popularly referred to as "torture till twelve".

Mlle Boulanger felt these classes developed her students' powers of concentration and extended their natural abilities by exposing them to tremendous stress. Selecting a student at random she would get him to play a piece from sight that he had never seen before, paying attention not only to the notes but to all the other notations in the score as well. She never allowed the students any time to hesitate before beginning in case they gained valuable seconds during which they could "study" the score before starting to play it. Walter quickly discovered it was the kind of exercise that exposed his strong and weak points clearly.

But being put under such stress so early in the morning was something difficult for him to get used to. It was always a tense situation and he would sit quietly, hoping he wouldn't be called upon until he had a chance to wake up. One morning though – and of course it was one on which he was feeling particularly groggy – she called him to the piano first.

Stumbling a little he made it to the stool and looked down to see if his feet were properly on the pedals. "What are you looking for?" Mlle Boulanger demanded imperiously. Instead of meekly apologizing, Walter was overwhelmed by his sense of the absurd. He said: "Well. Sometimes when I get up so early, I like to make sure I have the right shoe on the right foot."

A stunned silence in the salon. Walter waited for the lightning to flash and the thunder to roar. Why did he have to do things like that? With just a trace of a smile, Mlle Boulanger commented: "These Canadians. They're very strange. Very strange. Please continue."

Back in Poland after nearly a year in Paris: maybe he should stay here? really work hard? win the Chopin competition? become a national hero . . . ? That damn Canada Council rejecting his renewal. What did they think he'd been doing in Paris anyway? Still. He knew how to work now. That was the final thing he had needed to learn.

Dozing, on the Polish bus – on a specially arranged tour for foreign students – he fell into and out of his musical dreams. In his mind, sometimes, he could actually hear the way his composition would sound. Actually *hear* it – not just imagine it as he usually did while fully conscious – but hear it. A sure sign he was really bombed? Ah well. It was a traditional way to greet old friends. . . .

But no. He was quite sober. The bus had stopped. He was awake. And that beautiful girl bringing that tray of sandwiches onto the bus, one of the tour officials, was actually real and not

walter buczynski   113

a dream. And she was heading straight towards him. . . .

To Danuta, Walter seemed much too thin. (He weighed 110 pounds then, including his glasses.) As he smiled at her she felt like popping a sandwich into his mouth to fatten him up. They got into conversation and left the bus together at the end of the tour.

At the hotel a party was laid on. They danced. Walter kept drinking toasts of straight vodka. They kept dancing. Would his legs hold out? He asked her to go to a concert with him on Sunday. She told him she would if, when he got over his hangover, he could still remember. A glass of champagne finished him. His legs absolutely refused to move.

When Danuta said goodnight, he was motionless but grinning like a little gnome. She said, ''Remember next Sunday's concert if you can.'' His legs may have failed him, but his head was clear. Remember! He wasn't about to forget.

When he turned up she was only half-ready. She hadn't thought he'd come. Just a joker on the bus. But there he was. Her mother gave his sandals and baggy pants the once-over. The daughter was a professional secretary in the Tourist Department's offices – fluent in French, her native tongue, and all the Slavic languages as well. Her boyfriends were usually tall and handsome – and long past student days. What was this poor shrimp doing at the door? *A music student? And a foreigner? Aye! Aye!*

Danuta was twenty-four, three years younger than he was. What impressed him on that first date was her beautiful speech. Not just the sound of her voice but the logic and precision with which she used words.

They alternated between Polish and French. Danuta's family had gone back to Poland in 1948, from France where she was born. She was a specialist in Slavic and Romance languages, and was used to meeting people easily and making them feel comfortable. She had a good ear, but had never studied music much herself, except for a little piano. She, too, was a student, attending classes at night after working days in her office. And what about Canada? Was it a good place for composers and musicians there? Well . . . that depends. . . .

Besides her intelligence, Walter fell for her warmth and good humour – which brought out his own wit. He astonished her with his talent for puns and jokes in his second language. They were laughing every time they were together.

He tried to look his best. He took flowers with him. Six weeks he had known her. Her mother would likely throw a scene. Whew! He was nervous. How did his nose look? Not a bad job they did. The colds had gone away. He practised the traditional old phrases. It was all that subjunctive mood it was in. Something like, *would it be considered worthy that I might ask your daughter's hand perhaps to be held in mine in marriage. . . .*

Her mother came to the door. Her usual look up and down. He thrust the bouquet towards her. "I'd like to hold your daughter's hand . . . er, I mean I . . . . ." It was all right. She smiled, urged him to come in. Danuta came across the front room, smiling also. . . .

The Canada Council subsidiary grant came as a kind of wedding present. Only $500 but it meant he could just stretch out his time in Europe till the following spring.

They landed in Quebec on a hot first of July, 1962. Danuta was sick – two months pregnant with Christopher. The sea voyage had been miserable for her. Walter was suffering too. His appendix was inflamed. It was just a matter of time before he had to have it out. They stayed with brother Nicholas and the Buczynski family on Shaw Street. They were broke. Walter set out looking for work – hoping to delay the inevitable operation. But in August he had to be hospitalized.

He came out of hospital quickly, bent over for a few days until he had confidence the stitches would hold. Before they were taken out, he took advantage of his old teacher Earl Moss's offer to do some teaching at the Conservatory. Lucky – because, without insurance, he was $800 in the hole for the operation.

He took over thirty pupils, on a straight commission basis. If they were sick and didn't turn up, he didn't get paid. If he were sick and didn't turn up, same thing. After a while he had increased his pupil numbers to sixty-five. They just kept coming. Some of the original thirty he had inherited dropped out or went on elsewhere.

So much teaching was exhausting. He didn't practise, he did little composing, he did "nothing". They lived in "a crummy, little apartment with crazy Hungarians underneath who worked at night and slept during the day and were very rambunctious so I couldn't work."

Christopher was born in March 1963. Three weeks afterwards Danuta had to have a gall-bladder operation – the explanation of her pregnancy difficulties – and Walter was left holding the proverbial baby. His wife desperately needed to rest because her pregnancy had been difficult, and her first year in Canada emotionally trying for her. English was about the only language she didn't speak; so communication was virtually limited to her husband. Used to a fairly comfortable life in the security of her own family and professional career, she had a hard adjustment to make, made more difficult by her physical condition. Now she found she couldn't even pick up the telephone to take a message. She felt as if her arms and legs, but mostly her *head,* were cut off. Walter remembers that first year. "I thought I was going to go bonkers until Earl Moss took me aside. *You have to learn how to roll with the punches. If your student comes in prepared, that will make your lesson very enjoyable and you'll be prepared to give a lot of yourself. If he comes in unprepared, you teach him accordingly. Ease up, catch a few breaths while he's bumbling and stumbling around.*"

Walter started upping his fees to reduce his workload. His piano composition repertoire written during these three or four years until 1965, despite his difficulties, was still very respectable. It included *Le Temps du Jour avec Christophe,* a humorous, gentle piece written right after Christopher's birth, *Sonatina pour le Piano, Eight Preludes, Aria and Toccata, Suite one, two, three,* and most involving of all, *Amorphous,* a piece which suspends the listener's emotions between the large sound and silence spaces of its phrases. As with all Walter's pieces, the emotional idea must register for him to feel it is a success. Toronto critic Ralph Thomas, reviewing one of Walter Buczynski's own concerts on July 21, 1964, wrote: "His pieces *(Times of the Day with Christopher, Eight Preludes,* and *Aria and Toccata)* were sheer delights – cleverly constructed – poignant, and at all times interesting."

Every summer Walter had taken out a loan to tide him over the unpaid months until lessons began again. Once he had formed a trio (The Beaux Arts) with violinist Andrew Benack and cellist Mike Kilburn. They'd had a successful season including a stint at the Bahamas Festival in 1963.

Then in the fall of 1964 came the CBC. His experiences in Poland and working at the CBC were the two most important parts of his development as a composer and as a person. Digby Piers, an old colleague, and now a CBC producer, phoned him. A spot was open if he'd like to apply. He'd be responsible for writing the music and playing piano for "Playroom", an Ontario School Broadcast series. Would he want it? It paid $42.50 a show, three shows a week. He took it. It was a way of getting out of the hole.

Butterflies flutter by, macaroni slides down funny faces, trains whistle and chuff. . . . Every spare minute he orchestrated nearly one hour's music a week, as well as performing on the show. Writing it took less time than copying out all the parts. For that he soon developed speedy techniques, which helped later on with other work. Once an idea develops now he can write it up quickly.

Until that time he had lived by using his skills as an instrumentalist. For the first time he was making a living being . . . *yes . . . a composer.* It wasn't the highly creative avant-garde composing he knew he wanted to do, but it was practising his craft, being a professional. He put everything into it, refusing to improvise, for instance, as he might easily have done. In all the shows he wrote – perhaps three or four hundred – his producer questioned only one music cue.

Shuffling around his teaching hours at the Conservatory he managed to keep both jobs going at once. In a year he'd saved enough from the CBC alone to get out of the apartment and put money down on a house. Slowly he was cutting down his teaching and picking up on other small jobs at the CBC as well.

Strangely enough, he found he was doing more serious composing than before. From 1964 to 1966 while working on "Playroom", he wrote two short, orchestral works. *Three Thoughts for Orchestra* was commissioned by the CBC for the Toronto Symphony Orchestra, and this was followed shortly by *Triptych for Orchestra*. After these came *Four Arabesques and Dance for Flute and String Orchestra*. His ideas often come to him in imagistic forms, which he feels compelled to work out musically. *Triptych*, for instance, occurred to him while remembering the three-panelled altar paintings of mediaeval churches. The notion of conveying three different themes in a similar overall stylistic pattern began to intrigue him. Like the triptychs, his piece would not be in three entirely separate sections but would be hinged together into a single whole. In *Triptych* the three musical ideas are contained in the first minute as a kind of overture, which leads directly into a fragmentary section, a percussive section, and a final lyrical section. Only six minutes long, it contains dense, musical ideas without the unnecessary rhetoric of expansion, repetition, reversal or colouring.

His CBC work was essentially chamber music. It has always been easy for him to "hear" the effect of the limited number of instruments involved. Work for orchestra, though, especially in a modern idiom, is much more challenging. *You don't really "hear" it until the orchestra plays – you don't know what might happen when certain forces are going on at the same time – when it gets really "thick" and you're mixing red blue green purple black, it's like in painting – sometimes you don't know exactly what you'll get. If you want to do sound for sound's sake, O.K. . . . But it goes nowhere. You've got to have a thread, an idea, holding it TOGETHER. That's what communicates. It's just going to be random unless there's a concept there the audience can get. Otherwise they're going to get NOTHING. They'll just walk away – SO WHAT! SO WHAT!*

When Walter met Jane Beecroft, sister of the composer Norma

118   soundprints

Beecroft, the Buczynskis immediately struck up a friendship with the dark intense woman, who is an artist, a fine poet, and a frequent collaborator with musicians. Reading her poems, Walter was struck by thirteen of them, which he put to music and called *How Some Things Look.*

This collaboration led to two others in 1967: *Miłość/Love,* performed that year on commission for the Lyric Arts Trio for piano, flute and voice; and *Koinonia/Meeting of Minds* for tenor quartet, soprano, contralto, bass soloist and mixed choir. These works got him interested in the sound of the human voice as an element of composition – something used, also in 1967, for *Two French Love Poems.* This element is beginning to appear in Walter Buczynski's later work, not only as an instrumental force but as a *comic* force overlaying the music. In fact, one of his ideas is a comic opera with Danuta as collaborator on the libretto.

Another outcome of his CBC work has been two children's operas with words by Lilly Barnes: *Mr Rhinoceros* (1964) and *Do-Re-Mi* (1967). Perhaps because their work means years of dedication and poverty, not many composers have the kind of warm family life with children that the Buczynskis have. Walter's understanding of children crops up in these operettas as it does in *Le Temps du Jour avec Christophe,* and even in the comic aspects of later works. Perhaps because he has children, Walter doesn't consider these works any less ''meaningful''. ''I put myself into it one hundred per cent, as if it was any one of my works.''

He goes on to joke about how he played *God Save the Queen* at the old Crest Theatre to start the evening's performance. He did this for a month. It was a short walk away from his house and he'd accepted because they needed someone. ''I'll tell you something. When the people heard my *God Save the Queen,* they heard a performance! They didn't know whether they should cheer or not afterwards. I started off very quietly, very simply, then started to build until the whole auditorium was filled with this huge sound. I thought the people were going to come up and congratulate me afterwards! I felt I should give everybody a

walter buczynski 119

bill on the way out, you know. I enjoyed that. It was a lot of fun."

Other pieces written in Centennial Year included *Trio for Mandolin, Cello and Clarinet,* and *Sonata for Piano* and *Two and a Half Squares in a Circle* (for Jesse Kregal and his Timpani group). "Trio '67", written on commission for mandolin, cello and clarinet, explores the sound of the plucked mandolin (played by William Kuinka) in a contrasting dialogue with the bowed string and reedy wind sounds of the other instruments. With minimal means, Walter creates a composition with a wide range of sound colours. The plucked mandolin with its short, sharp ostinatos lends itself to the pointillistic "mode" that the piece is written in. The "conversation" approach in the scoring leaves the delicate sounds of the mandolin free to operate in uncluttered passages, thereby clearly defining it as the "lead" solo voice in the composition. Plucking also eliminates the Romantic era's attempt to bend the instrument into performing sustained notes by an unnatural vibrato using a plectrum. In this piece the mandolin's "natural" qualities come into their own.

The *Sonata for Piano,* also written in 1967, is one of Walter's favourite pieces. It explores areas of piano "sounds" that only a really skilled instrumentalist could have developed. For instance, its opening and closing great rolls of sound, which grow then fade like a monumental creative gesture in the founding of the universe, depend on sensing the sympathetic vibrations set up by clusters of low strings struck extremely rapidly, so that these sympathetic vibrations reduplicate themselves and slide on each other like tidal waves. A dense "white" sound emerges which, as it sweeps over the listener, reveals its inner patterns of percussive harmonics – rather like the visual sensation of embroidered, mediaeval altar cloths, whose complexity of design reveals itself more and more as the observer walks closer and closer, the large design element containing smaller ones which in turn contain their own structure, and so on.

But 1967, that tremendously productive year, cast a shadow into the next. When Gregory was born, Danuta was very happy. At that time her mother had come for a visit to Canada, and with her help, Danuta could cope. But three months afterwards, she realized she was pregnant again. Olenka (Alexandra), their winsome daughter, was born less than a year after Gregory. Danuta, still having trouble communicating, physically drained, and this time without her mother's help, found herself unable to cope. "What I needed was my mother!" She collapsed from the strain and was ordered by her doctor into hospital for three months. Desperately worried, and still working hard, Walter had to keep the house going. Olenka went to Poland to be with her grandmother for a time but the two small boys were a great demand on his emotional and physical resources. "Walter was everybody, Father, Mother, Lover, Friend, but he couldn't do everything. I guess it was the year I realized I could no longer be a child in any sense of the word at all. I needed a mother, so I had to become one."

In 1968 Walter wrote "NOTHING! Absolutely NOTHING!" (But changed a lot of diapers!)

Life slowly became normal again. Danuta was back, stronger and happier than she had ever been. The year had stalled his creative drive, however. It was hard to get going again – easier just to manage the ordinary affairs of his regular life – but a CBC commission gave him inspiration. Sitting at the piano in his living-room, where light from the bay window sparkled over the keys, he began working out a flashing sequence of ideas which evolved into a piece called *Iskry* (Polish: sparks). His creative fire was ready to be lit again.

John Weinzweig never formally taught Walter Buczynski, but liked what Walter wrote. About Weinzweig, Walter had stated in a magazine article, "Every note has a meaning, a direction." Like Weinzweig, Walter Buczynski believes a piece begins with a large "concept" that is then developed musically. "You can't just write sounds. You have to write thoughts. Music is a *language*." Also like Weinzweig, Buczynski is an independent thinker, open and tolerant of others' innovations, and unwilling to follow blindly current fads. The way he looks at it, the new experiments and discoveries are still waiting for someone to come along and put them all together. *First you have to get beyond the novelty fascination of new media and start reaching out into the real world.*

John Weinzweig had been persuading Walter that he should consider teaching at the Faculty of Music of the University of Toronto. It would give him the chance to teach composition theory to groups of gifted students; the intellectual resources of the Faculty would be open to him, and, while as a faculty member, with an assured salary, he would never be rich, at least he wouldn't have to worry.

Walter accepted the idea. His private students were a small number by then. The Faculty would only be able to offer him part-time teaching for his first year but it would be a start. . . .

At the same time as Walter joined the Faculty of Music on a part-time basis, Erindale College of the University of Toronto decided to hire ''in-residence'' people, who could give students advice on creative aspects of their intellectual development – help which they normally would be unable to obtain through their regular study programs. Soliciting advice from John Beckwith, soon to become Dean of the Faculty of Music, on who might fill the post of musician-composer, Principal J. Tuzo Wilson offered it to Walter Buczynski.

What does a ''musician-in-residence'' do? Before his first look at the College, Walter had been thinking about that question. Then he discovered that his office, which was placed at the far end of the preliminary building in a corridor later known as ''artists' alley'', consisted of a soundproof room with large double doors. Behind these doors was a brand new, Heintzman grand piano with a portable humidifier humming away to keep its belly wet. Just across the corridor was a large room of amphitheatre design that would make a good recital hall. Should he give recitals? His last recital had been five years ago. He'd been too busy to do the practising (and to revitalize his agent). Maybe he should start again. It was all there: the piano, time to practise, a place to perform, an audience to listen. . . .

His hands were sweating. *Whew! This was like Carnegie Hall.*

Performing had always made him nervous. This concert was no exception. And what a program he'd chosen for himself. "Well," he'd told Danuta, "I may as well go all the way." He'd thought of the educational side of the program as well as the aesthetic. That had made him choose the pieces. All sonatas. Beethoven's *No. 109,* Chopin's *Sonata in B Minor,* Roussel's *Sonatina,* and his own *Piano Sonata.* Would they like it? What would they feel about his experimental piece at the end? This was putting himself on the line all right. *That piano better be O.K. after getting jolted like that when they were shifting it. What if one of the pedals . . . ?*

Danuta arrived just in time. "Potam rece i nogi." Then he was by himself, walking to the piano, making his announcement about the pieces, adjusting the stool. *How about that pedal? O.K.? . . . PLAY!*

Assisting bright students from other fields who came to him with their interest in music began to give him confidence. He was one of the total academic community. He was exposing a wide range of people to good music, people who might never otherwise have become involved. And soon after he arrived at the College, Walter brought together interested students to form a band, which took over the gymnasium for a few hours a week. The music he wrote for them was in the contemporary mode but geared to their abilities.

He also began arranging concerts for other musicians to play at Erindale. The Public Lectures and Performing Arts Committees gave him a budget, which he used to bring to Erindale as wide a spectrum of music and musicians as possible, including Eugene Rittich (leading French horn of the Toronto Symphony Orchestra) and the Lyric Arts Trio. A hard-core following among students and faculty turned out regularly every two weeks and soon felt free to question and respond.

Walter, himself, gave several recitals during the two years he was there. Two of them were in collaboration with the writer of this book, Erindale's writer-in-residence. Since Walter was giving recitals again, he began playing Canadian music, some of which had been performed only rarely before. He gave two "all-Canadian'' concerts, one of them in the evening by firelight, in the Principal's Old English style mansion with its carved beams and marble fireplaces. The students, sitting on the floor, jammed the large rooms. During those two years he played in other colleges in Ontario as well, and gave two recitals for the CBC.

Both of these CBC performances featured new pieces he had written while at Erindale. The first was *Burlesque,* a humorous piece involving an internal dialogue that the pianist is having with himself about the trials of teaching and practising. This was coupled with the Roussel *Sonatina.* Then in 1972, he premiered *Zeroing-In #1,* an important work which marks the beginning of a new phase in his composing. This piece was coupled with a Bach *Partita,* because Bach's extraordinary use of counterpoint, which stretches not only the pianist's fingers but also his mind, was the inspiration for a different kind of counterpoint in *Zeroing-In #1,* that involves the pianist in singing and speaking while playing. Walter wanted to challenge the purely technical kind of piano-playing in which, as he puts it, ''You put a dime in the pianist's back pocket and the fingers begin to move.'' *Zeroing-In #1* also makes a comment on a statement being voiced by many modern composers that ''The piano is dead.'' In this piece, ''the piano is alive and well, and living in Toron-to!'' To prove it, the last ''movement'' uses electronic tape as well as live performance to give ''the impression of six-hand playing'' – a truly unique, dense, piano sound.

On a more serious level, the ''Zeroing-In'' series (five pieces by the time he left Erindale) is intended to involve the performers and the audience in the *process* of artistic creation, thus revealing the different kinds of musical elements with which the composer is working.

These pieces, some of them orchestral and stereophonic, force the audience to be aware of many things going on at once. Their structure tends to heighten consciousness by seducing the listener into applying all his intellectual as well as emotional resources in an effort to determine the shifting sound-patterns and their interactions – in the same way good poetry involves the senses as well as conducting the tongue. Walter Buczynski's position as composer/musician-in-residence gave his composing in this "Zeroing-In" series a dramatic edge, since he was consciously writing for a particular audience.

At the end of his two-year term at Erindale in 1972, Walter began teaching full-time at the Faculty of Music despite the fact that he, like many other composers, did not have a formal music degree. As a composer he allows each idea to generate its own form and to grow gradually into a unique work with its own structure. By working this way, Walter keeps himself from being labelled as a composer belonging to a definite school. His attempt, for instance, to keep the piano as a viable instrument in modern music presents enormous challenges that he is well aware of. But Walter Buczynski, never without a sense of humour, will continue to zero in on all the artistic problems ahead.

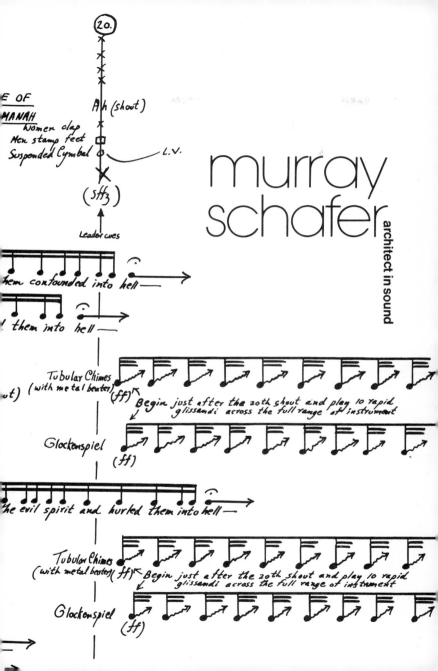

The new orchestra is the universe.

The piano concerto is a ghost in its midst.
And there is something spooky about the
institutions in which many pianos sit.

But let us forever cherish a few great pianos
in our company. Your treasure-museum is of
great beauty. You will not be forgotten, but
will forever enchant us with the reveries of
your memorable amours.

Tell us:

how Mozart tickled you
how Beethoven boisterously caroused with you
how Schumann kept you up late at night
how Chopin caressed you
how Liszt rode you like a wild stallion
how Debussy painted you blue
how Stravinsky mistook you for a stop clock
and how John Cage snapped your garters.

The above lines are from *The New Soundscape*
by R. Murray Schafer (BMI Canada, 1969).
Other quotations from Murray Schafer used as
glosses to the text are from *The Music of the
Environment,* prepared for the *UNESCO Journal of
World History; Ear Cleaning* (BMI, Canada, 1967);
Composer in the Classroom (BMI Canada, 1965);
Thoughts on Music Education, a paper which
was presented at the International Music Conference in Moscow, October 1971 (reprinted in *The
Canada Music Book,* Winter 1971); and *The Book
of Noise,* 1970 (privately printed with assistance
from Leon and Thea Koerner Foundation). Other
quotes in text are from a taped interview with
Murray Schafer unless otherwise stated.

urray Schafer himself had what he once called ''a mischievous love affair'' with the piano. The affair began at age six. It was a somewhat ambivalent relationship which, since he grew to detest the instrument, might have been a very temporary flirtation if his parents hadn't forced him to continue it. He stayed with it because he loved the music the piano made, and in a strange way, he loved the instrument itself, which looked to him somewhat like an overdecorated hearse. He managed to complete his degree after many years

---

Behold the new orchestra:
the sonic universe!
And the new musicians:
anyone and anything
that sounds!

---

to become an LRSM (Licentiate of the Royal Schools of Music, London, England), which is the only music degree he has.

He was born in Sarnia in 1933. At a very early age he lost an eye. Perhaps because of the visual bias of our culture this made him the butt of older boys' bullying. When he came out of school a gang would often be waiting with taunts, which were usually followed by his being beaten up. All this because he had a slightly different look about his eyes than they did. So

---

We will not argue for the priority of the ear.
Modern man, who seems to be in the process
of deafening himself apparently regards this
as a trivial mechanism. In the West the ear
has given way to the eye as the most impor-
tant gatherer of environmental information.
One of the most evident testaments of this
change is the way in which we have come to
imagine God. It was not until the Renaissance
that God became portraiture. Previously He
had been conceived as sound or vibration.

what were a few aches and bruises? He developed a wiry tough-
ness, which he showed while playing baseball and football, but
the greater part of his toughening-up to survive occurred in his
spirit. This ability to take unjust punishment to the most sensitive areas of one's being, he feels, is especially valuable to anyone aspiring to be a creative person. In the early years of an
artistic career one has to be able to endure punishment of various kinds "that would destroy the average human heart." He
learned to be able to recover spiritually and fight back. To keep
his inner person intact. He feels a kindred spirit to many creative
personalities – Joyce, for instance – whose careers were similarly influenced by rough childhoods due to their poor circumstances or physical disabilities. Picked on because they seem
weaker, such people often turn out to be more resilient than
their tormentors.

Murray stood "about eighth" in his classes at Humewood
Public School in Toronto. He doesn't remember it much at all.
However, his younger brother, Paul, who became a professor at
York University, went to a reunion there out of curiosity. On the
wall in one classroom was a display of distinguished ex-pupils
of Humewood who had achieved some fame or recognition.

---

*Warfare! As the machines whirl in the hearts
of our cities day and night, destroying,
erecting, destroying, the significant battle-
ground of the modern world has become the
neighbourhood* Blitzkrieg. *There may have
been a time when we thought this demolition
and reconstruction would be a temporary
inconvenience only, but we now realize it is
permanent and increasing. For the first time
in history, Constantin Doxiadis reminds us,
man is less safe in the heart of his city than
outside the city gates.
There are no regulations governing the
sound-levels permitted by construction or
demolition equipment in any Canadian city.*

Crowded among the sports-casters, athletes, and so on, was a silhouette of, sure enough, his brother Murray. Under the rather fuzzy photo of this internationally-known composer, music educator, researcher, and author was the caption, "Writer of background music and scripts for TV." Murray hardly remembers Humewood Public School and it remembers him only in a way which he feels reflects the primitive, cultural values of our society.

In later life he was to become a self-educated person whose private studies delved deep into disciplines as diverse as literature, language and science. Even during his early years he remembers doing a great deal of drawing and painting by himself, probably because of his father's influence.

His father's interest in the arts diminished with age, but he was "an immensely gifted man with little formal education". Professionally Murray's father functioned as an accountant in an oil company but at home he played "Moonlight Sonata" and other pieces on the piano although he had never had a music lesson in his life. Similarly, he sketched and painted pictures with untrained skill.

Murray Schafer never knew his grandparents, but looking back for some genetic inheritance to explain his own talents, he recalls that his mother's mother was an extremely musical person and perhaps the two strains, hers and his father's, collided in him fortuitously.

"The Tuning of the World" in which the earth
forms the body of an instrument across which
strings are stretched and are tuned by a divine
hand. We must try once again to find the
secret of that tuning.

His mother and father never raised the usual objections to his artistic ambitions. They encouraged his drawing and painting particularly, and Murray always assumed that was what he would do when he grew up. He kept this notion intact until he was eighteen.

Once in high school, in third form, Murray, aged fifteen or sixteen (this would be in 1948-49), was summoned to the guidance office for the usual counselling ritual.

MURRAY: I'd like to be a painter.

COUNSELLOR: A house-painter? Well . . . that's a very steady . . . .

MURRAY: No. I mean the other kind of painter.

COUNSELLOR: Oh. Well. You know there's lots of money in commercial art if you're prepared . . . .

As the students enter the class Schafer stands at the door motionless with a pile of paper in his hand and a sign pinned on his jacket reading: "Take paper. Write down the sounds you hear." The students entering take paper and record the sounds within and outside the room. A discussion follows to see how sound sensitive the students have been. Did they hear Schafer accidentally drop a Kleenex on the floor? And so forth. Two girls have engaged in periodic chatter. They were asked to read out the list of sounds they had heard. While each had recorded the sound of the other's voice, neither had heard her own voice. Pity.

MURRAY: No. I didn't mean a commercial artist.

COUNSELLOR: Oh. You mean painting portraits. Well. That's a . . . .

MURRAY: No. I want to be an abstract painter like Picasso. (Already he was thinking in terms of twentieth-century movements in the arts.)

COUNSELLOR: Now look here, young man. You're going to have a wife and family and you're going to have to look after them. How are you going to support them with the kind of money you're going to make from those dizzy paintings?

His parents seemed willing to leave as many doors open for

him as possible. Unlike the guidance counsellor his father never once asked him what he wanted to be.

Murray Schafer found high school "a revolting experience. I hated every moment of it. It was the most vile five years of my life." As he explains it, he was going through that mysterious and neurotic time of life called adolescence and didn't seem to be able to cover his neuroses as well as his classmates could. He did very badly. The only class he enjoyed was art.

There were no teachers he ever felt understood him, and the only time he remembers any special attention came when he did extremely well on some form of IQ test, while at the same time he ranked very close to the bottom of his class. "Teachers got flustered over the incongruity of that situation for a few days and then disappeared again." He was left to his own devices.

To fully-sighted people seeing stereoscopically ("in depth") is taken for granted. It's not something they have to think about.

What was the first sound heard: It was the
caress of the waters.

But just as "depth" in representative painting is the product of illusion and distortion on a two-dimensional surface to give the impression of three dimensions, so, too, to a person without stereoscopic vision, the landscape would be a perfectly flat pattern, if it were not seen with a continual (though obviously automatic) judgemental activity gained from past experience of all the other senses and personal mobility. In an ironic way such an activity increases sensibility by playing up the tactile senses.

It is too facile an explanation for the full range of his genius but many of Murray Schafer's activities and ideas bear the stamp of this influence. At that time in his life, trying as a receiver to judge the trajectory of a football in flight, or running a broken field, he was at a natural disadvantage, but as a strategist he had no equal. In fact, just after high school he coached teams of younger kids and in five years those teams scored 545 points and had only one touchdown scored against them. He used to correspond with coaches of large American teams and ask them about plays and strategies – a kind of initiative which he displayed later in life, especially in Europe where he entered into correspondence with and eventually visited Ezra Pound.

In Grade Eleven occurred one of the few great experiences of his high school life. He read, for the first time, A REAL BOOK! How, until then, he had avoided contact with any reading other than school texts, magazines and comic books still puzzles him. The book had been put on a required reading list for his English class. It was *Great Expectations* by Charles Dickens.

The novel affected him greatly. Perhaps it was because he could identify with the characters, or perhaps it was the evocative symbolism and compassionate tone; but for the first time he was completely fascinated by a work of literature. He realized he would never be the same again. He would read and allow himself to be affected by what he read.

The following year when the class studied Macbeth he memorized the whole play. He can still recite large chunks of it. From that time on he always did well in English Literature but not in English Composition.

English Composition was a very rigid and uninteresting subject. His final exam in Composition in Grade Twelve read, ''Write a sketch of an interesting person you have known.'' Unknown

---

The Musician is an Architect of Sounds
Throughout this essay I am going to treat the world soundscape as a macrocosmic musical composition. This is perhaps an unusual idea but I am going to nudge it forward relentlessly.

---

to his teachers Murray had been reading a great deal of philosophy himself. In an imaginative approach to the subject he wrote about a famous philosopher to whom he'd been introduced, and explained in the essay how this man had opened up to him great vistas of speculation concerning the mysteries of existence and human behaviour. The essay was returned marked FAILED and with a notation by the teacher: DON'T LIE.

The same year that he read *Great Expectations* was important for another reason. Still determined to be a visual artist he had been fixed in his musical tastes to the pop and jazz field and had little use for the classical music with which he had only been toying as a piano student. One beautiful May morning his father decided to take the family for a drive in the country to mark the end of winter. It was the family's first car and excitement was high. The car had a radio which his father turned on. Sun shining, air fresh, road unwinding. Then an orchestra began playing Beethoven's *Emperor Concerto*. The different sounds of the ensemble seemed to penetrate deep into his spirit. He was

---

The shore is symbolic of safety; the sea is symbolic of the unknown; the tension in our hearts is made audible in the crashing of breakers.

---

knocked cold. 'It was one of those 'Eureka!' moments. Suddenly I was hurled into the whole field of classical music.''

Managing to struggle to the end of Grade Twelve, Murray Schafer decided that was enough. His parents ''succumbed'' to the idea of his leaving with a Junior Matriculation diploma and the question of what professional training he should have cropped up again.

By this time his interest in music had increased, but still, at age eighteen, he felt he was more proficient in the visual arts. He moved into music little by little, however, since his studies at the Royal Conservatory of Music left it open for him to join a special course offered by the Faculty of Music of the University of Toronto. Later he was told that his choice was a happy

---

A character in one of Borges' stories dreads mirrors because they multiply men. The same might be said of radios.

---

one since with only one eye he wouldn't have developed into a really fine painter. He now feels that notion wasn't necessarily true since other artists, such as El Greco, whose myopia contributed to his famous elongated figures, were a success despite their handicap. Especially would his handicap not have mattered because of this century's developments in the visual arts: the integrity of two dimensional surfaces has been rescued from the perspective habits of previous times, and new concepts have liberated visual arts from both frame and pedestal.

In his music studies Murray Schafer at last encountered personalities who understood him and reached out to him. The three most significant teachers in his life were John Weinzweig, with whom he studied theory and composition; Alberto Guerrero, the Chilean master pianist, who also taught John Beckwith and Glenn Gould; and Greta Kraus, with whom he studied the harpsichord.

Arnold Walter, who was director of the Faculty of Music at that time, gave lectures in music history, which Murray Schafer enjoyed very much since they were filled with a lot of hard-core information and were well-organized. Murray's impression of Dr

---

The Acoustic Community
Community can be defined in many ways: as a political, geographical, religious or social entity. But I am about to propose that the ideal community may be defined advantageously along acoustic lines.

Walter, perhaps influenced by his continuing, private studies in literature and philosophy, was of a man with a "Spenglerian, gloomy kind of brooding quality, which persisted through his lectures."

Dr Walter and Murray Schafer encountered each other in another way, however. Murray at this time managed to "sneak into university" by registering for the Artist's Diploma Course which allowed people with a sketchy academic background to specialize in their instrument or other music interest. The course attempted to give a modicum of academic material in addition to the student's own specialty. These "academic" courses, unfortunately, were taken with the regular Bachelor of Music students. Murray was appalled in these classes by the "puerile attitudes of these people who were content to hug their professors and do whatever they had to do to get through their courses." He didn't conform to the norm, naturally, and ran into a great deal of trouble when he attempted to engage in what he felt was meaningful, intellectual dialogue. At the end of the year he was given a directive from Dr Walter to apologize in writing to various professors or to get out of the Faculty. He refused and, as he recalls, "was quietly expelled."

But the experience was useful to him. He resolved that he would have nothing to do with institutions or universities again but would devote himself to composing and his own intellectual development. His desire to educate himself was confirmed. Al-

---

I emphasize this again: In a class programmed for creativity the teacher must plan for his own extinction. And I will add parenthetically that it took me several years before I felt comfortable doing this.

---

ready while at the Faculty he had dropped in to various lectures and classes around the University, including some with Marshall McLuhan, with whose work Murray became very familiar. He was impressed by the fact McLuhan thought enough of his students to conduct classes in his own house. Murray went along for several sessions with a friend of his in Graduate English. McLuhan sat in a swivel chair opposite the fireplace in the middle of his living room. The students listened to some music "but mostly they listened to McLuhan himself." They asked questions and "the oracle of Delphi would revolve and fire back answers." They spoke about Roger Fry, James Joyce, Ezra Pound, and Clive Bell.

In later years Murray Schafer studied by himself the following subjects: Counterpoint, Latin, German (in which he is fluent), French and Italian ("I try to cope with these"), Arabic ("I found an Egyptian and learned it"), and a great body of philosophy and

literature (especially Joyce, Pound, Thomas Mann and Faulkner).
It was ten years before he could come to terms with having

Take, for instance, the telephone bell. Who
invented it? Certainly not a musician!

---

anything to do with universities and when he did so it was with
the personal resolve that he would ''try not to behave in the
way those people had behaved towards me. Fact is, I may have
been some sort of fringe character but I felt I was being dis-
criminated against in favour of an educational system that was
angled straight down the centre.''

His own teaching philosophy is diametrically opposed to his
experience as a student. He believes in the heuristic method, in
which the teacher sets problems or helps establish environments
and then lets students tackle them in their own time and at their
own pace in a spirit of joyful discovery. He has written a number of books which put forward his views. The first of these,
Composer in the Classroom (1965), resulted from an invitation

---

As time goes on Schafer gradually recedes
from the work and the class begins to take
over by making continual suggestions for
changes and additions. "This time you do this
and I'll do this", and so forth. One could not
say that the work was being brought to formal
consummation by this process; in fact, the
opposite often seemed to be the case. But like
the art of all non-literate societies, its vitality
rested precisely on its state of constant
revision.

---

to work with music students in schools in projects co-ordinated
by C. Laughton Bird for the North York Board of Education, and
a seminar sponsored by the Canada Council and organized by
John Adaskin of the Canadian Music Centre. Other books followed, as well as translations of much of his writing into Ger-

man and French. Murray Schafer has also written many articles, often very specialized, on topics such as "Ezra Pound and Music" and "A Basic Course (Source-Music of the Avant-Garde)". His education theories are given film exposure in a National Film Board documentary about him entitled *Bing Bang Boom,* which won first prize in the education film competition at the New York Film Festival in 1970.

Murray Schafer collaborated with Harry Somers and the Ontario Arts Council in developing *The Music Box, The Box of Noise* and similar teaching aids that use the same educational approaches. With *The Music Box,* students are able to explore a steamer-trunk full of noise-makers, books, pamphlets, question-cards, unusual early instruments and electronic tapes, filled with a full range of "electric" sounds that can be duplicated on a recorder and spliced to make "compositions".

Now in the Communications Centre at Simon Fraser University, Murray Schafer is engaged in the "World Soundscape Project" UNESCO has contributed $2,000 for equipment, and an

---

The Recovery of Positive Silence
In October 1969 the General Assembly of the International Music Council of Unesco passed a most interesting resolution.
We denounce unanimously the intolerable infringement of individual freedom and of the right of everyone to silence, because of the abusive use, in private and public places, of recorded or broadcast music.

---

award of $39,000 from the Canadian Donner Foundation has made it possible to hire research workers. Murray Schafer says his colleagues would probably be astonished to realize what a "dog-eared" formal education he has.

He had already started work on his first important composition while at the Faculty of Music in Toronto. It was completed in 1954 and showed the influences of that French group of early twentieth-century composers known as "Les Six", whose work he had studied intensely. Previous influences on him had been Mozart and then Debussy. He began work on this *Concerto for Harpsichord and Eight Wind Instruments* because of his interest in the harpsichord, an instrument he picked "because of its admirable clarity and because I wanted clear, clean lines." Recognizing that "for long, sustained melodies, however, it's rather useless," he explored its natural qualities as a contrapuntal instrument and its exciting possibilities for rhythm. For accompaniment he chose wind instruments rather than the usual strings because, again, of their "clean" sound in counterpoint and their tonal dynamics which he felt corresponded with the harpsichord's.

Probably the only important piece that could be said to mark a Neoclassic phase in Murray Schafer's composition, it encompassed a tremendous range of music "styles", reaching back to and beyond Scarlatti, and reaching as far into the twentieth-century as Les Six (especially Milhaud and Honegger, "with a little Stravinsky thrown in"). A very interesting feature of this piece is its rhythmic qualities. The rhythms are dominated in the first movement by a strange, crashing march tempo which seems to seek to thrash the life out of a skittering, showy toccata. In

---

Another useful exercise in asymmetrical rhythm is to construct messages in Morse code which must then be clapped rapidly in unison. Each student may also make up a "signature rhythm" on his own name. Poly-rhythm can be created by coupling these "signature rhythms", some double speed, half speed etc.

---

the second there is a slower, less frantic tempo which becomes biting and jerky with long rests, which begin to change the time values of the original, as if in anticipation of the gorgeous, rich "Mediterraneanized Baroque" of the last movement. The motifs of this finale are "woven into a rhythmic fabric of constantly changing tempi, which often change so rapidly that they become superimposed upon each other."

140 soundprints

As if he were in a hurry to dispense with as vast a spectrum of musical styles as possible in order to find his own voice, his next important piece, *The Minnelieder*, written the year when he was twenty-three and living in Vienna, was also "traditional".

Silence is the most potentialized feature of Western music. Because it is being lost, the composer today is more concerned with silence; he composes with it. Anton Webern moved composition to the brink of silence. The ecstasy of his music is enhanced by his sublime use of rests. By this means he produced hi-fi works in which diminutive but stunning musical gestures inhabit containers of stillness.

He still had a dislike of later twentieth-century composers such as Schoenberg and Webern and didn't "discover" them and others such as Bartok until, by age twenty-five, his ears had opened wider from the gamut of his European musical experiences.

He had made his way to Europe after his eviction from the Faculty of Music. To finance this, starting in the early spring of 1955, he went to work for nine months (a full season) on a Great Lakes oil tanker. His fascination with water and his beautiful poetic descriptions of it in his written work have much to do, perhaps, with his desire to be on, in, or around the "prime

---

All roads lead to water. Given the chance, probably men would live at the edge of the element, within earshot of its moods night and day. We wander from it but the departure is always temporary.

---

element" – one of the reasons why he lives in Vancouver and previously was in St John's.

Because there was little to spend it on, he saved enough

murray schafer   141

money to live in Vienna for nearly two years. He lived very cheaply there, spending only forty dollars a month for everything – including going to concerts.

In Toronto, from the age of nineteen he had dated a fellow student at the Conservatory, Phyllis Mailing, who was training as a vocalist. The piece he wrote in Vienna, *The Minnelieder,* was recorded by her later. During his time in Vienna they kept in touch, and she definitely influenced Murray's decision to write a long piece for the voice.

It is interesting to consider that while the voice can be raised to quite a loud level (about 75 decibels) at no time can it be raised beyond a level where it might endanger the ear (about 85-90 decibels).

Out of personal interest, he had been studying the Minnesingers (from the old German word for love, ''Minne''), who were similar to the Provençale Troubadours, about whom Pound had written so eloquently. Schafer set Minnesinger texts to music, which, completely unlike that of his harpsichord concerto, has long, undulating lines and which some critics feel has an affinity with the nobility and tragedy of Mahler's vocal line. Some of the songs are bright and happy, but most are sad since love unrequited or love lost, or love hopeless, was the mainspring of the courtly-love tradition.

Schafer himself feels this was ''the first work I would regard as a useful contribution to music.'' The traditional feeling of this piece now surprises him because he feels that a person of the age he was then, with the experience that he had already had in Europe, would have been writing in a much more avant-garde

---

Noise pollution results when man does not listen carefully. Noises are the sounds we have learned to ignore.

---

style – especially since he was not still isolated in a relatively provincial, musical tradition such as Toronto had during the early fifties.

After nearly two years in Vienna with sidetrips elsewhere, he made a fast dash back to Toronto, found it still distasteful, and headed back to Europe, this time focussing on London, with the help of a Canada Council scholarship. His tutor was the English composer, Peter Fricker, but he and Fricker had come to the arrangement that, instead of going through all the formal arabesques the Canada Council required, they would meet each other every Sunday morning and sit in the pub for a beer and a chat. They did this for a year.

Phyllis, too, arrived in Europe to study and Murray was in touch with her frequently.

He had already been writing various articles and now began doing freelance work for the CBC: interviews with musicians and composers as well as musical travelogues. One of these projects was later transcribed into his well-known book, *British Composers in Interview.* Especially interesting, in terms of the travelling involved, were his programs on the Balkans. In those days it was difficult to gain entry to countries such as Roumania, Hungary and Bulgaria, but unlike the sight-seeing of the camera-

---

In the rural soundscape sounds are generally
uncrowded, surrounded by pools of stillness.
For the farmer, the pioneer or the woodsman
the minutest sounds have significance. The
shepherd, for instance, can determine from
sheep bells the precise state of his flock.

---

wielder, which is often upsetting to people in more oral cultures, Murray's tape-recorded "sound-hearing" led him into interesting places and soundscapes. Once asked "What have been your most profound musical experiences?" he replied, "Listening to the peasant musicians of Roumania, Bulgaria and other truly musical societies such as one does not find here."

The most fascinating project he fell into, however, was an Ezra Pound opera. He had always enjoyed Pound's poetry and, while living in England, started a correspondence with him. In 1959 Pound had not long since been released from St Elizabeth's Hospital in Washington, DC (where he had been held as mentally unstable after the scandal of his activities in Italy during the Second World War). He was then living in a little castle in the Italian part of the Tyrolean Alps with his daughter and son-in-law, an Egyptologist. Murray had asked in a letter whether he could visit Pound to talk about music (particularly Pound's opera), which was Pound's other consuming interest besides his poetry. He had told Murray not to bother, but on one of his continental recording trips, Murray dropped in anyway.

On European trains the whistle is shrill, piping. In North America it is low, powerful, masculine, the utterance of a big engine with a heavy load. On the prairies – so flat that one can see the full train from engine to caboose, spread out like a stick across the horizon – the periodic whistlings resound like low haunting moans.

He found Pound all alone in the castle. The old man said, "So you've come!" Murray found his fabled generosity was in fact true. (Pound had supported a legion of starving artists in his younger days, and he had organized a fund-raising campaign to "get Tom Eliot out of the bank.") He was very willing to converse with Murray, really to converse, in a way which Murray had never found in other great men with whom he had come in contact. He actually found himself discussing with Ezra Pound a great range of subjects rather than simply listening to a monologue. Pound had always listened to young people.

Murray stayed with him there for a week. Every afternoon Pound would bring out books of poetry. He would read his own Odes and other poems from *The Cantos*. He also talked about his opera, which Murray later edited for the BBC – putting right some of the inconsistencies of the musical notations so that the musicians could perform it (the BBC production was in 1961).

Murray Schafer describes the work in his article, "Ezra Pound and Music", which was published in *The Canadian Music Journal* (Summer 1961) and subsequently anthologized in a book of critical essays on Pound, published in English, French and German.

Although discussion of the opera had been his main aim in visiting Pound, their conversations had ranged wide, and the great poet must have been impressed with Murray's sensitivity to literature and other subjects. On his last day Pound growled at him, "You're going back to London?"

MURRAY: Yes, I am.

POUND: Well. Here's sum readin' material for yuh.

He then handed the astonished composer an open, brown paper package. Murray realized it was the original, and probably only, draft of the last series of Cantos Pound had written. (Pound had been adding to them for almost fifty years.)

POUND: When yuh get back tuh London give 'em to Tom.

Tom, of course, was T. S. Eliot.

When Murray got back to London he took the manuscript over to Faber and Faber. He'd hoped to see "Tom" there, but the

---

The idea of a parish is also acoustic and it is defined by the range of the church bells. When you can no longer hear the church bells you have left the parish. Cockneydom is still defined as that area in East London within earshot of Bow Bells.

---

package was snatched out of his hands. Faber then wired Italy. Should they publish? Pound's family decided it would be better to withhold the manuscript for some time, since Pound would probably add to or complete the work further. As it turned out, he didn't do any more work on the Cantos before these were published (approximately ten years after Pound had intended them to be). Although they were not complete in a finished sense, Murray Schafer argues in his article on Pound that the

Cantos are substantially complete at any point in the same sense a Bach fugue is complete at any point. ("All you have to do is add a little pedal at the end and finish it off with a cadence.")

Voices of the Sea

At Oostende the strand is wide, with a
scarcely perceptible rake across to the hotels,
so that standing there one has the impression
that the sea in the distance is higher than
the beach and that sooner or later everything
will be lifted away to oblivion by an enormous
soft tidal wave. Totally otherwise is the
Adriatic at Trieste, where the mountains leap
into the ocean with an angular energy and
the angry fists of the waves bounce noisily off
rocks like India rubber balls.

The reason for this is that the Cantos are "a texture rather than a form, a procedure rather than a structure." Murray Schafer's connection with Ezra Pound continued, and launched him on a project to edit Pound's complete musical writings for a New York publisher.

Shortly after this visit to Pound, Murray Schafer and Phyllis Mailing were married in London, England. It was 1960. They came back to Canada together and this time decided to stay. Murray brought back with him the musical compositions he had completed during that time. These included an orchestral work, *In Memoriam,* dedicated to Alberto Guerrero, his old teacher who died in 1959.

The pieces he completed in 1961-62 while in Toronto began to indicate more clearly the direction his later works were to take. Dedicated to all political prisoners, *Canzoni for Prisoners,* written for full orchestra, reflects his growing concern with establishing a humane society. It is also important since it is the last in an array of compositions, each of which appears to be exploring one or another of the major concerns of twentieth-century music.

Andrée Desautels, in an article called "Canadian Composition" (in *Aspects of Music in Canada* edited by Dr Arnold Walter), expresses the nature of Murray Schafer's development this way: "Murray Schafer moved from polytonality *(Harpsichord Concerto* 1954) to pantonality *(In Memoriam: Alberto Guerrero* 1959); and finally, in *Protest and Incarceration* (1960) to atonality. In *Canzoni for Prisoners,* we find him experimenting with timbres, using sounds borrowed from percussion instruments, vibraphone, celesta, harp and piano: the pieces are veritable studies in sonority."

He had arrived by himself at each of these discoveries, and his true voice, rigorously trained, was at last free to resound through the endless possibilities of the sonic universe now open to him.

Aware of the vast quantities of interesting music that rarely had a chance to be played in a world music scene dominated by large symphonies, Murray Schafer decided to get involved

---

Had we recognized these things we could have predicted that the Church would have declined when the sound of the police siren (102 decibels) surpassed that of the church bell (83 decibels), just as the downfall of Islam was signalled when the first loudspeaker was attached to a minaret.

---

with an incredible project that has left its mark indelibly on Canadian music. It was the Ten Centuries Concert Series, which was founded to expose as wide an audience as possible to little-known music. Murray had struck a blow for little-played, interesting music once before and that was in his "final" year at the Faculty of Music in Toronto. With remarkable initiative he had got together with other young musicians to put on a concert of new works that was remembered for many years.

The Ten Centuries Concert Series went on for more than five years. The first two years it took most of Murray Schafer's time. There was the selection of the music and its scheduling to worry about, the hiring of musicians, and continual financial problems.

murray schafer 147

As its title suggests, the works would cover a range in time of ten centuries: from the present to the early beginnings of recorded composition. The ensembles required to play these works grew into a special group of highly versatile musicians, who later

---

It is possible to theorize that by 1967 the combined ramming of the 147,941 power chain saws produced that year, if operated simultaneously, could cover about one-tenth of Canada's 9,222,977 square kilometers with their sound. As chain saws bang thrillingly throughout the forests of the world the contemporary woodsman loses all contact with the music of nature.

---

acted as a talent pool from which could be drawn the instrumentalists needed for the New Music Concert Series. This series, which succeeded the Ten Centuries, had as its president Norma Beecroft, who had been a contemporary of Murray's at the Conservatory.

By this time Phyllis Mailing, his wife, was giving recitals. Her mezzo-soprano voice, of exceptional quality and range, was bound to continue influencing Murray's vocal music as it had in *The Minnelieder.* ''Of course she's influenced me very much . . . the fact that I spent so much time in the presence of a person who has such a beautiful voice. And simply listening to this creature practising in the background was very useful to me in learning what the voice could do – what was suitable for the voice and what was unsuitable. I could try out techniques with her and of course all of my major vocal works were all written for her voice . . . they suit her range, her tessatura; they suit her rich and dramatic quality.''

Murray's concern with the whole notion of ''depth'' as a musical phenomenon reveals itself clearly for the first time in *Five Studies on Texts by Prudentius.* Written with Phyllis in mind just before they had left England, it is set for mezzo-soprano and four flutes. The stereophonic effect of depth is achieved by

148 soundprints

placing each flute in one of the four corners of the concert hall with the singer on stage. The voice is called on to leap from low A to high C sharp, a range of well over two octaves, as well as to perform swooping glissandos, bird-like trills and sometimes

---

The Hi-Fi and the Lo-Fi Soundscape
A hi-fi system is one possessing a favourable signal to noise ratio. The hi-fi soundscape is one in which discrete sounds can be heard clearly because of the low ambient noise level. The country is generally more hi-fi than the city; night more than day; ancient times more than modern. In a hi-fi soundscape even the slightest disturbance can communicate interesting or vital information. The human ear is alert, like that of an animal.

---

lullaby-like hums or percussive staccatos. The patterns of stereophony set up by the flutes create different spacial effects, which correspond to five short, poetic captions. Murray explains that these captions were originally commentaries ''to accompany scenes from the Bible painted on the walls of churches during the Middle Ages. The five episodes here form a miniature Bible in themselves, from the story of Adam and Eve to the revelation of St John with the birth of Christ appearing in the centre.'' The spacial effect created for ''Adam and Eve'' is centrifugal to suggest the serpent; in ''Moses has Received the Law'' it is diagonal; and in ''The City of Bethlehem'' it moves in concentric circles suggesting the centrality of Bethlehem in space and time and the central position of Christ in the Christian religion. ''The middle canon is to be regarded as the focal point of the entire composition.''

But despite his growing recognition as a composer and a driving force for the betterment of music, the mushy-in-winter, unromantic-in-summer, noisy city of Toronto, whose waters were hardly ever seen, could not keep him once the Ten Centuries Concert Series had become a going concern. In 1963 he accepted an invitation to become artist-in-residence at Memorial University in St John's – where the rocky fingers of Newfoundland's shores reached out towards Europe.

At Memorial, the President indicated that he didn't want Mur-

---

It ought to be possible to calculate the rise in ambient city noise fairly accurately by studying the intensities of emergency warning systems over the years. In Mozart's days, Vienna was quiet enough that fire signals were given by the shouts of a scout mounted atop St Steven's Cathedral.

---

ray to feel he had to become involved in teaching. The position was one designed to allow him as much time to do his own work as possible. But Murray soon gathered together interested students and formed an amateur brass consort that gave concerts of all the Baroque and Renaissance brass music that Murray could find and interpret for them. His contact with students also helped him with the basic concepts of *Composer in the*

The class is asked to discuss how they would set each word of the following Latin sentence to music.

Deposuit potentes de sede et exaltavit humiles.

(He hath put down the mighty from their seats and exalted the humble and meek.)

The phrase is rich in emotional qualities and each word demands special attention. The communal setting might be notated on the board in notes or merely by means of curved or angular lines. Only after the psychographic curve of each word has been discussed in detail does the instructor play a recording of Bach's setting of these words from the Magnificat in D.

Classroom, which grew out of his teaching experiences with primary and high school music students in Toronto during the summer of 1964.

Now situated by the ever-changing sea and freed from the necessity to spend a great deal of time at things other than his composing, Murray Schafer began to establish the working pattern that was to characterize the formation of his later works. This pattern exists independently of commissions, although it is flexible enough to include them as long as they don't establish conditions that run counter to his own desires. Murray has described that pattern as being like a "bow" of a thought that extends over years. He likes to tie his life together with large-limbed ideas that he can project out on. The idea of "the big work" seems to offer a continuum that contrasts with and at the same time anchors his "general splattering of energies" in many different fields. There are really three substantially complete works that have grown in this way: the bilingual TV opera, *Loving/Toi;* the mystical triptych, *Lustro;* and the stagework, *Patria.*

Each of these works has an almost frightening originality and depth of concept. One of them has been performed as a whole work: *Loving* on CBC TV in May 1966. And there are similar plans for *Lustro.* Bits and pieces of all of them have been "leaked" over the years — masquerading as commissions, chamber music pieces or choral works. Both *Lustro* and *Patria* have three parts. The second part of *Patria,* well-known as *Requiems for the Party-Girl,* has had many performances, including one by the New York Philharmonic and another at Ontario's Stratford Music Festival, both in 1972.

Loving reflects Murray's long-held notion that the separate arts will soon fuse together, not in "a Hollywood mishmash" but in a "counterpointing synaesthesis". Although it is called an opera it has few of the opera's traditional characteristics. In his program notes, he explains: "There are no characters . . . but there are what we might call 'attitudes'. In the game of love the masculine or feminine psyche adopts certain poses or 'attitudes' to confront the opposite sex . . . three feminine 'attitudes' in particular dominate *Loving* . . . they are given the rather picturesque names of Vanity, Ishtar and Modesty. . . . The drama unfolds on many different levels, both conscious and

---

The ocean of our ancestors is reproduced in the watery womb of our mother and is chemically related to it. Ocean and Mother. In the dark liquid of ocean the relentless masses of water pushed past the first sonar ear. As the ear of the foetus turns in its amniotic fluid, it too is tuned to the lap and gurgle of water.

---

unconscious. . . . The whole attempt is to produce a 'presence' rather than a story. . . . In darkness, in silence, in the mysteries of its structure, *Loving* creates the nocturnal texture of a love affair – its sounds, allusions, moods and spells. . . . The concern was to explore the world between speech and song – between meaning and sound – and to give the work a constellation of verbal and musical relationships, of which only a portion would exist on the surface and much would be subconscious or dreamlike.''

The production was a very difficult affair since the direction aspects of the camerawork were extremely complicated. Pierre

---

Schizophonia
The Greek prefix schizo *means split, separated. Schizophonia refers to the split between an original sound and its electro-acoustical transmission or reproduction. It is another twentieth-century development.*

Mercure, a composer and CBC producer of outstanding talent that Murray describes as ''the only guiding spirit musical television has ever had in this country,'' took on the formidable job and the unique challenges it created.

But before the production was completed Pierre Mercure was killed in a car accident – a tragedy for the country. Two important sections, consequently, were not completed; but the production of *Loving* went on as scheduled early in 1966, once on the CBC French network (as *Toi*) and once on the CBC English network, with those parts omitted. Television viewers had not seen anything quite like *Loving's* sensuality and surrealism before, and their reactions were immediate. Most critics praised it, though some were completely bemused by the revolutionary procedures they had witnessed.

Murray Schafer's text was composed of haunting poetic fragments of speech that echo repeatedly through the arias, discourses and dialogues: "I came to you naked and neighbourly . . . The rampage of your loins upon my loins . . . You nameless and tousled . . . I surrender myself to the cabinet-work of sleep" . . . and so on.

Voices grow into and out of the sounds of the instruments. In Ishtar's aria the instruments follow and imitate the voice. The effect is a blurring of the distinctions between human and artificial soundsources, as the whole piece is a blurring of one sense into another: "locating the points where their nerve endings touch." Bernini's beautiful sculpture of Daphne in the process of being turned into a laurel tree in her strange escape from Apollo, the Greek god of music, is perhaps the closest visual parallel to reflect the many kinds of blends and metamorphoses in the sounds, sights and textures of *Loving*. Four separate arias from *Loving* are: "The Geography of Eros" (1964), "Ishtar" (1965), "Modesty" (1965), and "Vanity" (1965). The whole work took over a year of constant effort to complete. It has never been graced with a stage performance by an opera company.

"Requiems for the Party-Girl", again a work written for Phyllis Mailing, is the second part of *Patria*, the still unfinished, vast stage work that Murray began to conceive as long ago as 1966. It started out as a centennial commission for the CBC. "'Requiems for the Party-Girl' documents the mental collapse and suicide of a young woman . . . she is the prototype of those strange, harlequinesque creatures one meets occasionally at parties, beneath whose furious demonstrations of gregariousness and *joie de vivre* one detects obscure signs of terror and alienation.''

Such a difficult, sensational kind of subject matter could have been a disaster if the music and words had tried to beat the listener over the head with the pity of it all; but the text is kept brief, and the music subtle, so that in only one or two places does the piece begin to slip into bathos. At times the voice and instruments shift in subtle quarter tones, creating unusual sounds that jar and vibrate. Especially is this so in the treatment of the

---

In a lo-fi soundscape individual acoustic signals are obscured in an overdense population of sounds.
There is cross-talk on all the channels, and in order for the most ordinary sounds to be heard they have to be monstrously amplified. In the ultimate lo-fi soundscape the signal to noise ratio is 1 to 1 and it is no longer possible to know what, if anything, is to be listened to.

---

phrase ''the voices of the world'' which occurs in those high-tension moments before the trigger is pulled, and the word ''requiem'', repeated and repeated, tumbles, bounces, writhes and collapses in a jangle of bells which sound the Party Girl's deathknell.

Raymond Ericson, reviewing the New York Philharmonic's production for the *New York Times* in 1972, writes: ''It is a haunting work, written with extraordinary expressivity and theatrical power. It is serial in style, but every note seems to have emotional value, and the vocal line uses all the modern devices in a beautifully lyrical way. Phyllis Mailing, the Canadian mezzo for whom it was written, sang superbly with Mr Maderna conducting. One can only hope the composer finishes his opera soon.''

By the time *Requiems* was completed Murray had gained recognition for his writings and views on music education and other music subjects not only in Canada but also in the USA,

England, Australia, Germany and Austria. In a review of *Composer in the Classroom,* Irving Lowens writing in the *Washington Star* urged ''read it. . . . This is a work you can read in an hour, but you will remember it gratefully for the rest of your life.'' Similar acclaim greeted *Ear Cleaning,* published in 1967.

Exercises, Discussions, Assignments
Assume you have been mute for a long time.
Try to feel the vibrancy of cutting the air with
pristine sound – the terrifying freedom of the
ictus.

In 1965 Murray Schafer had moved from sea to sea across Canada to take up a similar position in the new Simon Fraser University in Burnaby, British Columbia, a suburb of Vancouver. The two large works, *Loving* and *Patria,* seem mostly to concern the inner psyche – exploring those Joycean, Kafkaesque dreamworlds. But because of his involvement in the intellectual communities at St John's and Simon Fraser, Murray was inevitably going to become more concerned with social problems, to which he would have to respond. This ''outward'' looking composing had taken life previously in smaller forms such as the *Protest and Incarceration* and *Canzoni for Prisoners. Gita,* commissioned

Acoustic Design III: Quiet Groves and Times
The huge noises of our civilization are the
result of imperialistic ambitions. Territorial
expansion has always been one of our aims.
Just as we refuse to leave a space of our
environment uncultivated, unmastered, so too
we have refused to leave an acoustic space
quiet and unpunctured by sound.

by the Fromm Foundation for the Tanglewood Festival in 1967, looks into the problem of attaining serenity of spirit, and is a setting of a portion of the *Bhagavad Gita* in the original Sanskrit. A widely noticed success, it led indirectly to *Lustro,* his third "big" work.

Gita was followed by *Threnody* (commissioned by the Royal Conservatory of Music Toronto Alumni for the Vancouver Junior Symphony Orchestra). This blazing piece uses snatches of eye-witness accounts of the bombing of Nagasaki as its text and leaves the audience moved almost to tears at its conclusion. Robert Sunter of the Vancouver *Sun* wrote: "*Threnody* left most of the 600 people in North Vancouver's Centennial Theatre furtively dabbing their eyes. . . . Schafer drew some extraordinary sounds which had powerful emotional and dramatic impact."

Murray was also at work as consultant on two Expo pavilions: he composed music for the Kaleidoscope Pavilion and also for the Man and Life Pavilion. About this time he began research for his book on the sound environment, *The New Soundscape,* since his position in the Communications Centre at Simon Fraser was leading him and his colleagues into new fields of exploration. The Sonic Research Studio, which Murray Schafer built up, is one of the best in North America. Still in the process of construction, and often fragmented by student protest, the University was a hectic place to be. In *The Book of Noise,* Murray Schafer points out that the University's soundscape had as much

Noise and Anarchy
Noise is disorderly sound, without purpose.
As such it may be compared with disorderly
or confused action – i.e. anarchy. . . .
A certain university in Western Canada has
been in existence for five years. During that
time it has been undergoing constant further
construction. The profile of this construction
noise . . . has infected the entire campus for
this period . . . .
It will not be irrelevant to suggest an un-
studied correlation between the general chaos
and noise level of this campus and its social
disorders.

to do with these problems as anything else. Relief from this pile-up of commissions, projects, and lectures came in the form of a Canada Council award in 1968.

With the award Murray received a notice that travel money was available. It asked where he would like to go during the term of the award. He hadn't thought about travelling again, but he was intrigued by the idea that someone would finance a journey which might bring him new sounds and experiences in any corner of the world he wished. Reaching for a globe of the

---

(Parenthetically, I might mention one memorable drive from Pergamum to Aescelapion, a distance of seven kilometers, during which my chauffeur blew his horn 289 times at nothing in particular.) Vancouver has a monstrous horn mounted on top of one of its highest buildings, which signals twelve o'clock by playing the opening phrase of the Canadian national anthem. One block away this sound is 96 dB – 100 dB.

---

world he spun it to a place approximately halfway round from Vancouver and stuck out his finger. Teheran. It was a lucky choice.

Since before *Gita* he had become interested in mediaeval Eastern mysticism, particularly *Sufism* or *Sofism* (from Arabic: çūfī, man of wool). This Moslem sect, which originated in the eighth century, in its Persian form embraces a pantheistic philosophy which sees God in everything. A Sudanese splinter sect of the eighteenth century, the Dervishes (from Persian, *darvesh,* poor) gave rise to the group known as the ''whirling dervishes'' who dance themselves into a religious trance.

But his fascination had not only been with Eastern philosophy but also its architecture. ''To see the architecture of Persepolis was one of the big moments of my life.'' This was the city through which paraded Tamburlaine the Great, who had risen from humble shepherd to ruler of a vast Tartar empire. Then there were the incredible mosques at Isphahan. ''The Shah Abbas mosque there is the most beautiful, intact building I have ever seen.''

In the Middle East it is the area over which
the muezzin's voice can be heard as he
announces the call to prayer from the minaret.
Aristotle somewhere gives 5,000 as the size of
the ideal community and cites as evidence the
`fact that one man can address that number
of people with his naked voice – but not more.

The direct results of this trip were ''Music for the Morning of the World'' and ''Divan i Shams i Tabriz'', which together with ''Beyond the Great Gate of Light'' (completed in 1972), form *Lustro*. The first two of these pieces have as their generating points texts by Jalal ed-Din Rumi, the mystical poet.

Divan i Shams i Tabriz (a title borrowed from Rumi's work), a great orchestral piece, has one of the most stunning beginnings in music. The ''ictus'', that point where silence is shattered with the onset of sound, has been a particular point of study by Murray Schafer, who symbolizes it in many ways in his writings, sometimes as life denying death or light overwhelming darkness.

In creating you are given one free gesture.
After that comes the discipline of establishing
relationships. We are still on that point of
free gesture. Only for that instant until we
slice into sound do we feel terrifyingly free.

Here the ictus explodes over the audience in an incredible rush of textured noise. First, as the vividly graphic score indicates, an anvil is struck, a chain crashes to the floor; set free, the soul dashes in terror through a universe sizzling with chaos; the singers wail ''Where shall I flee?'' The piece blends taped and live sounds in a stereophonic quest symbolic of search, change, synthesis, resolution and final peace. There are taped sounds

158 soundprints

suggesting wind, rain and thunder. Unusual instruments produce exactly the right effects: as well as the chain and anvil they include a bicycle-wheel clacker and a series of gongs.

These last are particularly appropriate to the piece with their long, deep resonances which help to establish an Eastern sound environment. The struck brass sounds of such instruments have

---

There is another solution, a solution so elementary it needs stress. Respect quiet. Keep silent. Keep silent like the points of a compass, like the mystic, like the forest. Close eyes, sit attentively, and rediscover the merest sounds of all. It is an oriental solution . . . but whoever practises it will be the true inheritor of whatever replaces the present.

---

a quality which Western classical music had difficulty integrating into its close measures. Only in the limited range and functions of the cymbal do we find such sounds (safely imprisoned and controlled) in the classical orchestra.

If there is any ''signature'' by which Murray Schafer's work can be instantly recognized, it is this fascination with the ictus and with dense envelopes of colliding sounds out of which rings a single, strong tone as if it were a stone that flew true – order demanding passage through chaos.

''For beauty is nothing but the beginning of terror.'' This motto from Rainer Maria Rilke defines Murray's approach to his work. ''Music that speaks directly; music that is created perilously; music created by composers who risk everything; dangerous music.''

His last, huge work has to do with Theseus and the Labyrinth. Begun as he was still finishing *Patria,* it looms before him as a project of many years standing with a maze of possibilities.

Murray Schafer regards himself as a composer first. If any contribution of his will have a lasting life he expects and hopes it will be his compositions. The other things he is involved in, and there are a great many, he sees as ephemeral, even the

World Soundscape Project and his campaigning against noise pollution. These are things he feels cannot be easily bequeathed in substance to future generations. Composition fulfils his ambition to have progeny.

In the imagination of the Prophets the end of the world was to be signalled by a mighty din, a din more ferocious than the loudest sound they could imagine; more ferocious than any known storm, more outrageous than any thunder. Modern man is beginning to produce in his cities an environment more ferocious than any known storms and with his aircraft more outrageous than any thunder. It is disconcerting to realize that we may be stupid enough to fulfil this prophecy.

Composing is at the generating centre of his life and commands all his talents and energies. His gorgeously rendered scores with their swirls, swoops and inner designs are works of art in themselves and have been so used. Literary and graphics magazines have also printed them. When his books, too, require illustration, he usually does most of this himself.

When the Japanese calligrapher paints, he sits motionless for what seems to be an eternity; then he picks up his brush and with a deft movement of the wrist, fastens a perfect symbol to the page. He has been mentally mastering that movement for a lifetime. He doesn't fumble.

In a more abstract direction, his compositions influence or reflect the concerns of his research, teaching and philosophy. And they bind his life chronologically with a sense of purpose and order. "I hate composing, because it's the hardest thing to do. I brood for a long time over a new work. As it begins to take shape I get more and more short-tempered, more and more moody until finally I know I can't put it off any longer but must sit down and start writing. This is what I mean about facing the real spiritual problems, I mean the religious problems, because, in its deepest sense, religion is concerned with placing order above and against chaos; and this is also what art is all about. The creator gave us this instinct when he made us, when he made the universe; and he made it move in this precise and very elegant way.''

CREDITS

From *Trialogue* / 2
Gilbert A. Milne, Toronto / 3
From *Kuyas*, Berandol Music Ltd / 31
From *The Sun Dance* / 54
Robert Lansdale, Etobicoke / 55
John Reeves, Toronto / 78
From *Contrasts for Six Composers* / 79
Laing Portraits, Toronto / 102
From *A Work for Dance* / 103
Frisco Photo, Montreal / 126
From *In Search of Zoroaster* / 127

Book design / Mary Cserepy

First date indicates when work was composed. Date after publisher's name indicates date of publication. Published scores, of course, are available from the publisher. (BMI Canada's catalogue was purchased by Berandol Music Ltd. in 1969.) Most of the unpublished scores listed here, as well as published scores, may be readily borrowed on request from the lending library of the Canadian Music Centre, Toronto, Ontario.

John Weinzweig

Band

Band – Hut Sketches (1943)
Round Dance, arranged by Howard Cable (1950; Leeds 1965)

Chamber Music

String Quartet No. 1 (1937)
Fanfare (1943)
Sonata, violin and piano (1941; Oxford 1953)
Intermissions for Flute and Oboe (1943; Southern 1964)
String Quartet No. 2 (1946)
Cello Sonata (Israel) (1949)
String Quartet No. 3 (1962)
Woodwind Quintet (1963-64)
Clarinet Quartet, educational (1964-65; Leeds 1970)
Around the Stage in Twenty-Five Minutes During Which a Variety of Instruments Are Struck (1970)

Choral

To the Lands Over Yonder (1945; Frederick Harris 1953)
Am Yisrael Chai! (1952; Leeds 1964)

Orchestra with Soloist

A Tale of Tuamotu, bassoon and orchestra (1939)
Divertimento No. 1, flute and string orchestra (1945-46; Boosey and Hawkes 1950)
Divertimento No. 2, oboe and string orchestra (1948; Boosey and Hawkes 1950)

Violin Concerto (1951-54)
Divertimento No. 3, bassoon and string orchestra (1959-60; Leeds 1966)
Divertimento No. 5, trumpet, trombone and winds (1961; Leeds 1969)
Concerto for Piano and Orchestra (1965-66)
Concerto for Harp and Chamber Orchestra (1967; Leeds 1969)
Divertimento No. 4, clarinet and string orchestra (1968)
Divertimento No. 6, soprano, alto or tenor saxophone and string orchestra (1972)

Orchestral

Spectre (1928)
Legend (1937)
The Whirling Dwarf (1937)
The Enchanted Hill (1938)
Suite (1938)
Symphony (1940)
Rhapsody for Orchestra (1941)
Interlude in an Artist's Life (1943; Leeds 1961)
Our Canada (1943)
Prelude to a New Day (1944)
Edge of the World (1946; Leeds 1967)
Round Dance (1950)
Symphonic Ode (1958; Leeds 1962)
Dummiyah (Silence) (1969)

Organ

Improvisations on an Indian Tune (1942)

Piano

Suite No. 1 (1939; "Waltzling" in *Fourteen Pieces by Canadian Composers*, Frederick Harris 1955)

Piano Sonata (1950)

Suite No. 2 (1950; Oxford 1965)

Stage

Mackenzie River (1941)

West Wind (1942)

The Great Canadian Shield (1945)

Turner Valley (1945)

Red Ear of Corn, ballet suite (1948-49)

Vocal

Of Time, Rain and The World (1947)

Dance of the Massadah (1951)

Wine of Peace (1957; CMC study score 1957)

Trialogue (1971)

Harry Somers

Chamber Music

Duo, two violins (1943)

First String Quartet (1943)

Mime, violin and piano (1947)

Rhapsody for Violin and Piano (1948)

Woodwind Quintet (1948)

Second String Quartet (1949-50)

Trio for Flute, Violin and Cello (1950)

Sonata No. 1, violin and piano (1953; BMI 1968)

Sonata No. 2, violin and piano (1955; BMI 1968)

Third String Quartet (1959)

Sonata for Guitar (1959; E. C. Kerby/Caveat)

Theme for Variations (1964; BMI 1966)

Etching – The Vollard Suite, flute solo (1964; Ricordi 1969)

Choral

Where Do We Stand, Oh Lord? (1955; BMI 1955)

Two Songs for the Coming of Spring (1957; BMI 1957)

God the Master of This Scene (1962; Oxford 1964)

Gloria (1964; Oxford 1964)

The Wonder Song (1964; BMI 1964)

Crucifixion (1968)

Five Songs of the Newfoundland Outports (1969; G.V. Thompson/Chanteclair 1969)

Orchestral

Sketches for Orchestra (1946)

First Piano Concerto (1947)

Scherzo for Strings (1947; AMP 1948)

North Country Suite, for string orchestra (1948; BMI 1960)

Suite for Harp and Chamber Orchestra (1949; BMI 1959)

Symphony No. 1 (1951)

Lament and Primeval (for piano 1946, orchestrated 1952)

Passacaglia and Fugue for Orchestra (1954; BMI 1958)

Little Suite for String Orchestra on Canadian Folk Songs (1955; BMI 1956)

Second Piano Concerto (1956)

Fantasia for Orchestra (1958; BMI 1962)

Lyric for Orchestra (1960; BMI 1963)

Symphony for Woodwinds, Brass and Percussion (1961)

Movement for Orchestra (1962; Ricordi 1964)

Five Concepts for Orchestra (1961; BMI 1964)

Stereophony for Orchestra (1963; E. C. Kerby/Caveat 1972)

The Picasso Suite (1964; Ricordi 1969)

Piano

Strangeness of Heart (1942; BMI 1947)

Two Etudes (1943)

Flights of Fancy (1944)

A Fragment (1944)

Three Sonnets (1945; BMI 1948)
Testament of Youth (First Piano Sonata) (1945)
Second Piano Sonata (1946)
Solitudes (1947)
Four Primitives (1949)
Third Piano Sonata (1950)
Fourth Piano Sonata (1950)
12 × 12 – Fugues for Piano (1951; BMI 1959; No. 1 only, Frederick Harris 1955)
Fifth Piano Sonata (1957)

Stage
The Fool (1953)
The Homeless Ones, operetta in three scenes (1955)
Faces of Canada, incidental music (1956)
The Fisherman and His Soul, ballet by Grant Strate (1956)
Ballad, ballet by Grant Strate (1958)
The House of Atreus (1963)
Louis Riel (1967)

Vocal
Stillness (1942)
Three Songs (1946)
A Bunch of Rowan (1947; BMI 1948)
Three Simple Songs (1953)
Conversation Piece (1955; BMI 1957)
Twelve Miniatures for Voice and Instrumental Trio (1964; BMI 1965)
Evocations (1966; BMI 1968)
Kuyas (1967; Berandol 1971)
Improvisation (1969)
Five Songs for Dark Voice (1956; Berandol 1972)
Voiceplay (1971)

John Beckwith

Chamber Music
Five Pieces for Brass Trio (1951)
Five Pieces for Flute Duet (1951; BMI 1962)
Four Pieces for Bassoon Duet (1951)
Quartet for Woodwind Instruments (1951)
Three Studies for String Trio (1955-56)
Circle, with Tangents (1967; BMI 1968)
Taking a Stand (1972)

Choral
Jonah (1963; BMI 1969)
The Trumpets of Summer (1964)
Sharon Fragments (1966; Waterloo 1966)
Place of Meeting (1966-67)
The Sun Dance (1968)
Three Blessings (1968; BMI 1968)
Gas! (1969)
1838 (1970; Novello 1970)

Collage (with James Reaney)
A Message to Winnipeg (1960)
Twelve Letters to a Small Town (1961)
Wednesday's Child (1962)
Canada Dash, Canada Dot (1965-67)

Orchestra with Soloist
Concerto Fantasy, piano and orchestra (1958-59)
Concertino, horn and strings (1963)

Orchestral
Montage (1953; rescored 1955)
Music for Dancing (1948; orchestrated 1959; BMI 1961)
Fall Scene and Fair Dance (1956; BMI 1957)
Flower Variations and Wheels (1962)

Piano
Four Conceits (1945-48)
Music for Dancing (1948)
The Music Room (1951; Frederick Harris 1955)
Novelette (1951; BMI 1954)
Six Mobiles (1959; BMI 1960)
Interval Studies (1962; BMI 1962)
Suite on Old Tunes (1966; BMI 1967)
Variation Piquant sur la "Toronto Opera House Waltz" (1967)

New Mobiles (1971)

Stage

Night Blooming Cereus, an opera (1953-58)

The Killdeer, incidental music (1959)

The Shivaree, an opera (in progress from 1965)

Vocal

Five Lyrics of the T'ang Dynasty (1947; BMI 1949)

The Great Lakes Suite (1949)

Four Songs to Poems by Edith Sitwell (1949)

Four Songs to Poems by e.e. cummings (1950)

Two songs to poems by Colleen Thibaudeau (1949 and 1950)

Four Songs from Ben Jonson's "Volpone" (1961; BMI 1967)

A Chaucer Suite (1962)

Ten English Rhymes (1963; BMI 1964)

Four Love Songs (1969; Berandol 1970)

Five Songs from Canadian Folk Collections (1970; Waterloo 1970)

Norma Beecroft

Chamber Music

Tre Pezzi Brevi (1960-61; Universal Edition 1962)

Contrasts for Six Performers (1962)

Elegy, and Two Went to Sleep (1967)

Rasas (1968-69)

Choral

The Hollow Men (1956)

The Living Flame of Love (1967; Waterloo 1969)

Electronic

Undersea Fantasy (1967; Composer, tape)

Electronic, Chorus, Orchestra

From Dreams of Brass (1963-64; in preparation by Leeds)

Orchestral

Two Movements for Orchestra (1957-58)

Fantasy for Strings (1958)

Improvvisazioni Concertanti No. 1, flute and orchestra (1961; in preparation by Leeds)

Pièce Concertante No. 1 (1966)

Improvvisazioni Concertanti No. 2 (1971; in preparation by Leeds)

Walter Buczynski

Chamber Music

Sonata for Violin and Piano (1953)

Trio for Violin, Cello and Piano (1953)

String Quartet (1955)

Sonata for Violin and Piano (1955)

Suite for Woodwind Quintet (1955)

Nonette (1955)

Divertimento for Four Solo Instruments (1957)

Suite for String Trio (1959)

Chorale and Five Variations (1960)

Elegy for Violin and Piano (1963)

Six Miniatures for String Quartet (1963)

Four Corners of Gregory, guitar (1966)

Trio for Mandolin, Cello and Clarinet (1967)

Two and a Half Squares in a Circle (1967)

Chamber Opera

From the Buczynski Book of The Living (1972)

Dance

A Work for Dance (1970)

Opera for Children

Mr Rhinoceros and His Musicians (1964)

Do-Re-Mi, operetta (1967)

Orchestral

Adagio and Allegro for Classical Orchestra (1958)

Three Thoughts for Orchestra (1964)

Triptych for Orchestra (1964)

Beztitula for Piano and Orchestra (1964)

Iskry / Sparks (1969)

Seven Miniatures for Orchestra (1970)

Zeroing-In #2 / Distractions and Then (1971)

Text for Orchestra and Other Soloists (1971)

Zeroing-In #3 (1972)

Zeroing-In #4 / Innards and Outards (1972)

Organ

Five Atmospheres for Organ Solo (1966)

Piano

Three Preludes (1956)

Three Improvisations (1957)

Three Romantic Pieces (1957-58)

Le Temps du Jour avec Christophe (1963)

Aria and Toccata (1963)

Eight Preludes (1963)

Sonatine pour le Piano (1964)

Suite pour le piano (one, two, three) (1964)

Amorphous (1964)

Suite de la Radio pour le Piano (1965)

Sonata for Piano (1967)

Burlesque for Piano, pianist's voice and tape (1970)

Zeroing-In #1 (1971)

Zeroing-In #5, a dictionary of mannerisms (1972)

Piano for Children

Four Pieces for Middle Grades (1965)

Seven Pieces for Small Children (1965)

Ten Piano Pieces for Children (1965)

Eight Epigrams for Young Pianists (1965; Boosey and Hawkes 1969)

Three Piano Pieces (1965; Frederick Harris 1970)

String Orchestra

Children's Pieces for Strings (1964-65)

Four Arabesques and Dance for Flute and String Orchestra (1964)

Four Movements for Piano and Strings (1969)

Vocal

Seven Songs for Soprano and Piano (1952)

Cycle of Three Songs for Soprano and Piano (1954)

Four Poems of Walter de la Mare (1955)

How Some Things Look (voice and piano 1966; soprano and instrumental ensemble 1967)

Two French Love Poems (1967)

Miłość / Love (1967)

Koinonia / Meeting of Minds (1967)

R. Murray Schafer

Chamber Music

Concerto for Harpsichord and Eight Wind Instruments (1954)

Sonatina for Flute and Harpsichord or Piano (1958)

Five Studies on Texts by Prudentius (1962; BMI 1965)

Requiems for the Party-Girl, arias from Patria (1966; BMI 1967)

Minimusic (1969; Universal Edition 1971)

String Quartet (1970; Universal Edition 1972)

The Enchantress (1972)

Choral

Four Songs on Texts by Tagore (1962)

Gita (1967; Universal Edition 1972)

Threnody for Youth Orchestra (1966; revised 1967; Berandol 1970)

Epitaph for Moonlight (1968; Berandol 1969, Universal Edition 1971)

Yeow and Pax (1969)

Miniwanka or The Moments of Water (1971)

From the Tibetan Book of the Dead (1968; Universal Edition 1972)

In Search of Zoroaster (1971)

Tehillah (1972)

Orchestral

In Memoriam: Alberto Guerrero (1959)

Canzoni for Prisoners (1961-62)

Untitled Composition (1963)

Statement in Blue (1964; BMI 1966, Universal Edition 1971)

Son of Heldenleben (1968; Universal Edition 1972)

Divan i Shams i Tabriz, from Lustro (1969; revised 1970)

No Longer Than Ten Minutes (1970; revised 1972)

Beyond the Great Gate of Light, from Lustro (1972)

Stage

Loving/Toi, an opera (1966)

Patria (1972, incomplete)

Tone Poem

Okeanos (a quadraphonic tone poem dealing with the sounds of the sea, in collaboration with Brian Fawcett and Bruce Davis, CBC 1972)

Vocal

The Minnelieder (1956; Berandol 1970)

Kinderlieder (1958)

Protest and Incarceration (1960)

Brébeuf, a cantata (1961)

Music for the Morning of the World, from Lustro (1970; Universal Edition 1972)

Sappho (1970)

INDEX

169

Date Due

FORM 109